Perfect
Brain Training

Philip J Carter

Philip Carter is the author or co-author of over
one hundred titles for adults and children,
including *Take the IQ Challenge* and *The Ultimate
IQ Book*. His books have been translated
into several languages including Chinese,
Japanese, Korean, Russian, German, Spanish,
Portuguese, Hungarian and Rumanian. He lives in
Huddersfield, West Yorkshire.

Other titles in the *Perfect* series

Perfect
Brain Training

Philip J Carter

BOOKS

Published by Random House Books 2009

2 4 6 8 10 9 7 5 3 1

First published in Great Britain in 2009 by
Random House Books
Random House, 20 '
London SW1V 2SA

www.rbooks.co.uk

Addresses for comp;
can be found at: ww

The Random House

A CIP catalogue rec(

ISBN 9781847945549

The Random House Group Limited supports The Forest Stewardship
Council (FSC), the leading international forest certification organisation.
All our titles that are printed on Greenpeace approved FSC certified
paper carry the FSC logo. Our paper procurement policy can be found
at: www.rbooks.co.uk/environment

Typeset by Puzzle Press Limited, www.puzzlepress.co.uk

Printed in the UK by CPI Bookmark, Croydon CR0 4TD

Contents

Introduction

The human brain is our most valuable asset, but for many of us it is the part of our body we take most for granted.

Our brain is the control centre for virtually every vital activity necessary for survival including movement, sleep, hunger and thirst. It gives rise to our perceptions and memory, and it shapes our speech, skills, thoughts and feelings. It also receives and processes signals that are sent to it from other parts of the body and from sources external to the body. Yet it is perhaps the part of the body that we tend to neglect the most.

Despite the enormous capacity of the human brain, we only use on average 3% of our potential brainpower. This is the amount of information available to us consciously and the rest is locked within our subconscious mind. There is, therefore, a great deal of potential for each of us to expand our brainpower considerably.

Our brain needs care and exercise in the same way as other parts of the body. In the same way that we eat the right foods to keep our heart healthy, we moisturize our skin to keep it from drying out and we walk, swim, cycle or jog to keep our bodies in good shape, there are Brain Training exercises we can do to enhance the performance of our brain and increase quickness of thought.

This book sets out to show that by regular practise on different types of tests and puzzles each one of us has the capacity to maximise our brainpower on different types of brain activity.

Most of us take our brain for granted believing there is little we can do to improve our brain power. This, however, is not the case and most experts are in agreement that it is possible to considerably increase our brain power and utilise our brain potential to a much greater degree, and the use of puzzles and tests can be of great value in giving our brain a much needed workout.

To quote just two examples from recent years, research has shown that in Japan the playing of computer games has increased the average IQ of schoolchildren, and in America puzzle books have been supplied to elderly residents of residential homes in order to aid mental stimulation.

We have in the past few decades become much more aware of the importance of the human brain, the way it functions, its relationship to our own body and its relationship to the outside world. Despite this we still know so little about the human brain that there is a fear factor – the fear of the unknown that we do not even dare to think or talk about. If we are able to overcome this obstacle and develop the belief that we have the capability of not only warding off brain degeneration but of strengthening our brainpower, then any improvement will be that much easier for us to achieve.

There is a subtle difference between puzzles and problems. A puzzle is set by another person, and it has a solution which is already known to that person.

A problem, on the other hand, arises in life. It is not set artificially and there is not an answer already known to someone else. There is no right answer; some solutions may be better than others.

Both puzzles and problems can produce their own rewards. The successful solution of a problem, for example, achieves a worthwhile goal and, as well as their recreational value, puzzles stretch and exercise the mind and frequently involve different, original and creative thought processes which enable us to tackle the real problems of life with renewed vigour and confidence.

This book consists of ten mental workouts and five progress tests. Each mental workout is structured to exercise seven different aspects of mental activity:

1. Thinking Quickly

Agility of mind is the ability to think quickly and react instinctively to certain situations. In all the exercises in this category a Target Time is suggested.

2. Thinking Verbally

Life today is all about communicating properly, and to do this effectively we need to endeavour to increase our level of verbal skills and dexterity.

3. Thinking Numerically

The subject of mathematics can be challenging, fascinating, confusing and frustrating, but once you have developed an interest in the science of numbers, a whole new world is opened up as you discover their many characteristics and patterns.

We all require some numerical skills in our lives, whether it is to calculate our weekly shopping bill or to budget how to use our monthly income, but for many people mathematics is a subject they regard as being too difficult when confronted by what are considered to be its higher branches. When broken down and analysed, and explained in layman's terms, however, many of these aspects can be readily understood by those of us with only a rudimentary grasp of the subject.

In keeping with many of the puzzles throughout this book, some of the number puzzles in the Brain Workouts, are challenging, but deliberately so as the more you practise on this type of puzzle, the more you will come to understand the methodology and thought processes necessary to solve them and the more proficient you will become at arriving at the correct solution.

4. Thinking Logically

A definition of logical is analytical or deductive, and this definition can be applied to someone who is capable of reasoning, or using reason, in an orderly, cogent fashion.

There is no specialized knowledge of mathematics or vocabulary required in order to solve questions of pure logic, just the ability to think clearly and analytically, and follow a common sense reasoning process.

5. Thinking Laterally and Creatively

The word *lateral* means: of or relating to the side, away from the median axis. Lateral thinking is a method of solving a problem by attempting to look at that problem from many angles rather than search for a direct head-on solution. It, therefore, involves the need to think outside the box and develop a degree of creative, innovative thinking, which seeks to change our natural and traditional perceptions, concepts and ideas. By developing this type of thinking we greatly increase our ability to solve problems that face us that we might not otherwise solve.

To solve the puzzles of this nature it is necessary to think laterally and creatively and, in many cases, look for solutions that may not seem apparent on first inspection.

6. Thinking Spatially

The ability being investigated with spatial puzzles is how well a person is able to identify patterns and meaning from what might appear at first glance random or very complex information.

The definition of spatial is pertaining to space, and spatial abilities mean the perceptual and cognitive abilities that enable a person to deal with spatial relations.

Typical spatial reasoning puzzles may take the form of a series of shapes or diagrams from which you have to pick the odd one out, or identify which should come next in a sequence from a set of alternatives, or choose from a set of alternatives which diagram will complete an analogy. They are also designed not just to test your powers of logic and your ability to deal with problems in a structured and analytical way, but also to make you think laterally and creatively.

Both creativity and spatial aptitude involves quite different thought processes to those which determine verbal or numerical aptitude and it is quite common for people who excel at numerical and verbal puzzles to perform equally badly on spatial aptitude puzzles and tests and vice versa.

This is because the left side of the human brain is analytical and functions in a sequential and logical fashion and is the side which controls language, academic studies and rationality. The right side of the brain is creative and intuitive and leads, for example, to the birth of ideas for works of art and music and is the side of the brain which determines how well we are able to adapt to tests of spatial aptitude. As many people have some degree of brain bias, they thus perform better on puzzles which involve thought processes controlled by the stronger side of their brain.

7. Memory

Memory is the process of storing and retrieving information in the brain. It is this process of memory that is central to our learning and thinking.

Human beings are continually learning throughout their lifetime. Only some of this massive volume of information is selected and stored in the brain, and is available for recall later when required. Learning is the acquisition of new knowledge, and memory is the retention of this knowledge. The combination of learning and memory, therefore, is the basis of all our knowledge and abilities. It is what enables us to consider the past, exist in the present and plan for the future. Its importance and power should not be underestimated.

Every part of our life relies to some extent on memory and is what enables us to walk, study, relax, communicate and play; in fact whatever function we perform some sort of memory process is at work.

It is also accepted that the more we use our memory, the better it becomes. It is, therefore, important to stimulate the memory by using it to the utmost, learning new skills and using memory enhancing techniques.

The memory puzzles in this book are designed to test and assess your powers of memory and at the same time to assist you in improving your memory by developing your powers of concentration, and disciplining yourself to fix your mind on the subject being studied.

Whilst the book is structured to include ten distinct brain workouts, above all the puzzles and exercise are primarily designed to provide fun and entertainment throughout.

It is, therefore, entirely up to you how you wish to use the book - either to attempt one workout at a time, or simply dip into the book at random and attempt whichever of the many questions takes your fancy. It is, however, recommended that to derive maximum benefit from the workouts you pace yourself to attempt a number of puzzles each day at a time which is most convenient to you, for example an hour each morning may be convenient, and when you are feeling least pressured, also that the puzzles you attempt be as varied a selection as possible at each session.

In addition to the ten workouts a further five short tests are included throughout the book which provide the opportunity to monitor your progress as you work your way through the workouts. The tests are of approximately equal length and difficulty level and at the end of the book a graph is provided on which to plot your progress. It is recommended that in order to monitor your progress as accurately as possible that the five tests are attempted in the order in which they appear in the book.

THINKING QUICKLY

In each of the following ten questions identify the symbol which appears the most and enter the number of times it appears together with a sketch of the symbol in the box provided.

For example:

☺ ○ ↕ ☺ ♦ ♣ ♪ ♀ ♫ ♪ ♣ ♥ ☼ ☺ ♪ ‡ ↕ ∏ ↕ ♪ ♣ ♀ | | |

Answer:

| ♪ | 4 |

The symbol that appears most times is ♪ and it appears four times.

This is a speed test against the clock.

You have a target time of 12 minutes in which to complete the 10 questions.

1.

⊓ ☺ ▲ ♦ ‡ ☼ ♀ ∏ ∑ ♫ £ & ☼ ♀ ↕ ▲ ☺ ☼ ‡ | | |

2.

£ ♪ ♀ ☺ ♥ ∏ ‡ ▼ ✚ ‡ ♪ £ ✚ ♫ ∑ ♪ & | | |

3.

♦ ↕ ▲ ☼ ♀ ☺ ♥ ∏ ▼ £ ♥ ‡ ♫ ∑ & ✚ ♪ | | |

4.

◻Ω♫♣♫—╫♫£Ω€@#&Ω♣╪—▼Ω—@ ▢▢

5.

∑♪♥◻╫£€#◻&♣╪▼—♫@Ω$ΨΠ ▢▢

6.

≠ F ¥ © @ ♣ ◻ ® μ ¥ © @ — ♫ © ▼ ▢▢

7.

♫♪♦♥♣♠♂♀☼☺◀▼♦╪∑€Θβ#$ ▢▢

8.

∑╪€β$∑╪βΘ€β€╪$β╪€∑β$#╪☺β☺ ▢▢

9.

╞ ⌐⌐ ⌐⌐ ⌐⌐ ╙ ╙ ╘ ¬ ¬ ¬ ╘ ╓ ╓ F ▢▢

10.

♫♦♂☼☺◙▼☺▲♪♥♣☺◀♫☼♂£Ω£ ▢▢

THINKING VERBALLY

1.
Scramblegram

Four six-letter words all on the theme of fruit have been jumbled.
Solve the four anagrams and enter the answers next to each
anagram, reading from left to right or top to bottom.

Next transfer the letters in the shaded squares to the keyword box
below to find a fifth word (of eight letters) on the same theme.

	N	O	M	A	D	S	
O							C
N							I
A							N
G							Q
E							U
R							E
	H	E	R	C	R	Y	

KEYWORD

2.
A familiar phrase has been sliced up into three letter bits which
have then been placed in the wrong order. Can you reconstruct the
phrase?

ASI   EAM   RYL   EVE

IKE   EMO   HAV

The phrase is: _____

3.
Solve the four clues to find four six-letter words. The three starred
letters in each answer are identical, and spell out a three-letter
word.

* * * _ _ _   acid/pertaining to vinegar

_ * * * _ _   cluster of flowers along a main stem

_ _ * * * _   arranged with gaps between

_ _ _ * * *   threat

4.
Insert the name of an animal onto the bottom row to complete six
three-letter words reading downwards:

T	S	B	R	D	F
U	E	I	I	U	A

THINKING NUMERICALLY

Complete the Number Matrix Puzzles

In each puzzle several numbers are missing. The same number pattern is occurring in each row of numbers across and a different pattern is occurring in each column of numbers down. You have to decide, by looking across each row and down each column, just what pattern of numbers is occurring and fill in the missing numbers.

For example:

2	3	5	4
5	6	8	7
4	5	7	6
6	7	9	8

In the above grid, the numbers in each row across are progressing +1, +2, -1; in each column down they are progressing +3, -1, +2.

1.

1		2		7
	13		17	15
7	11			
		12	19	
6		7		

2.

	5			30	
8		27	34		31
	24			49	
11					
	23		45		42
		44	51	54	

THINKING LOGICALLY

1.

What comes next in the above sequence?

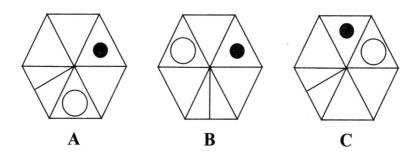

A   B   C

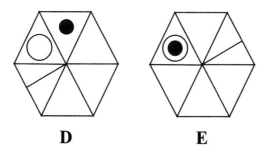

D   E

THINKING LOGICALLY

2.

⊥ ━ ⊥ ╫ ━ ⊥ ╫ ┬ ━ ⊥ ╫ ┬ ╫ ━ ⊥

Which two symbols continue the sequence?

a. ⊥ ╫   b. ╫ ┬

c. ┬ ╫   d. ╫ ⊥   e. ┬ ╫

3.

♠ ♣ ♥ ♦ ← ♠ ♣ ♥ ↑ ♠ ♣ → ♠ ↓ ♠ ♣ ← ♠ ♣ ♥ ↑ ♠ ♣ ♥

Which two symbols continue the sequence?

a. ← ♠   b. ↑ ♣

c. → ♣   d. ♦ →

4.

●○●●○●●●○●●●●━○●○○●○○○●○○○○━●○●●○●●●○●●●

Which three symbols continue the sequence?

a. ━○●   b. ○━●

c. ●●━   d. ●━○

THINKING LATERALLY AND CREATIVELY

1.

Draw the four missing symbols in the grid below in accordance with the rules of logic already established.

Σ	♫	§	#	Σ
#			Σ	#
§			♫	§
♫	Σ	#	§	♫
Σ	♫	§	#	Σ

2.

F ? R A A R N I C S E

What letter should replace the question mark?

3.

Which is the odd number out?

7142	3186	3688
9455	7284	5153

4.
What sequence can be added to the words

RODS, BLOW, ALAS, CANE and SAVE

To produce five new words?

5.
If the score of eight dice totals 40, what is the average of the scores on the opposite sides?

THINKING SPATIALLY

1.
Which is the odd one out?

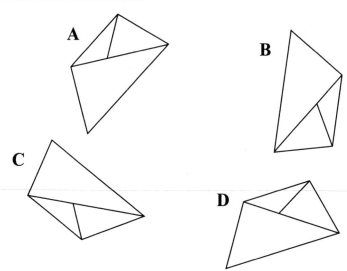

2.
How many more discs of exactly the same size as the one already placed are needed to completely cover the square?

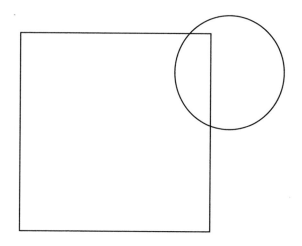

THINKING SPATIALLY

3.
Which three of the pieces below can be fitted together to form a perfect square?

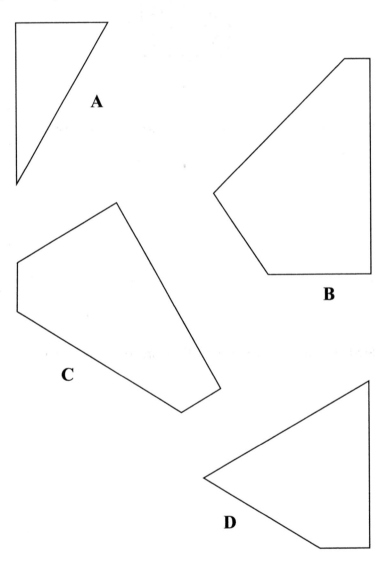

MEMORY

1.

O	X	X
O	X	O
X	O	X

Study the above for 20 seconds, then turn to the next page.

2.

→ ↕ ↓ ← ↓ ↔

Study the above for 20 seconds, then turn to the next page.

MEMORY

1.
Which of the following have you just looked at?

X	X	O
O	X	O
X	O	X

O	O	X
X	O	O
O	X	X

O	X	X
O	X	X
X	O	X

X	O	X
X	O	X
O	X	O

O	X	X
O	X	O
X	O	X

O	X	O
X	O	X
O	X	X

When you have an answer, turn back to see if you are correct.

2.
Which of the following have you just looked at?

← ↑ ↔ ↑ ↓ →

↑ ↓ ↔ ↑ → ↕

→ ↕ ↓ ← ↓ ↔

→ ↕ ↑ → ← ↔

When you have an answer, turn back to see if you are correct.

THINKING QUICKLY

1.
Word/Symbol Speed Exercise

In each question find the longest word that is spelled out by
substituting letters for symbols in accordance with the key below.

♪	Ω	£	♣	♂	Σ	Π	‡	&	#	▲	¶
H	O	Y	P	E	C	W	L	A	T	N	I

Example:

♣	♂	#	Σ	&	▲	¶	▲	♂	#	¶	♂

Answer: CANINE
The words PET, CAN, NINE, NET and TIE also appear, but
CANINE is the longest word that appears in the grid below.

♣	♂	#	Σ	&	▲	¶	▲	♂	#	¶	♂
P	E	T	C	A	N	I	N	E	T	I	E

Target time eight minutes:

1.
&	‡	‡	¶	♣	Σ	♪	&	‡	Ω	Π	▲

2.
Σ	♣	‡	Ω	£	&	‡	#	Ω	¶	‡	£

3.	¶	#	♫	♂	Σ	▲	#	Ω	Π	▲	♂	Π

4.	▲	♂	Π	#	&	♯	♂	▲	#	¶	&	£

5.	Π	&	Σ	♂	♯	&	Σ	♫	♂	Σ	Ω	▲

2.
Letter/Number Rearrangement Exercise

Arrange the letters in forward alphabetical order followed by the numbers in descending order. Target time eight minutes:

i.   K Y 7 F 2 5 B J S T 4 6

ii. 9 D B E 8 2 S G Z L

iii. 7 G U M R 3 8 L A E C 5 2 H

iv. T 6 9 J U 4 D S Z 3 B M A 8

v.   P R 7 3 G X D 4 6 S Y 2 C U W

THINKING VERBALLY

1.
Word Change Exercise

Two-Word Change

Exchange the position of two words only in each of the sentences below so that they then make complete sense:

1.
The electricity is passed to the engine leads by the top of the rotor arm, driven by the plug crankshaft.

2.
Florida is an example of a large landmass as it is surrounded on three sides by water but still attached to a larger peninsula.

3.
Reputedly made in Staffordshire, it is originally named after Toby Philpot, a character in an 18th-century ballad.

Three-Word Change

Exchange the position of three words only in each of the sentences below so that they then make complete sense:

4.
Thermistors are used in electric filaments and large motors to stop lamp currents flowing through them when they are initially turned on.

5.
A consumed resource, such as coal or oil, that takes thousands or millions of years to form and can, therefore not be natural once it is replaced is referred to as a non-renewable resource.

2.
Crossword

Across

1 Earlier in time (5)

6 1960s abstractionism (2,3)

7 Relating to Switzerland (5)

8 Youthful (5)

9 Fragment (5)

12 Subsequent (5)

13 Dwelling unit (5)

14 The present age (5)

Down

1 Complementary ticket (4)

2 Travelling from place to place (9)

3 Flushed (4)

4 Soaked (9)

5 Male deer (4)

9 So much (4)

10 Secret plan (4)

11 Cry of an ass (4)

THINKING NUMERICALLY

1.
Addition Exercise

Complete the table by adding the numbers along the top to the numbers down the side. For example: referring to the numbers already inserted; 6 + 15 = 21, 31 + 9 = 40 and 19 + 7 = 26.

Try to complete the exercise in your head without the use of a calculator or pencil and paper.

Target time 10 minutes:

+	7	15	9	23
8				
13				
6		21		
17				
26				
31			40	
19	26			

2.

5 9 6 3 8 2 7 5 9 1 7 6 4 8 2 9 7 6

What is the total of all the odd numbers that are immediately followed by an even number in the list above?

3.
A farmer has 260 yards of fencing and wishes to enclose a rectangular area of the **greatest** possible size. What will be its area?

4.

6219 (81)   **4829 (77)**   **7421 (?)**

What number should replace the question mark?

5.
I completed a journey by rail, bus and taxi. If the train fare cost £17.55, the taxi fare cost £9.75 less than the train fare and the bus fare cost £6.20 less than the taxi fare, how much did the total journey cost me?

6.
A market stall owner takes delivery of a box of apples and to his consternation finds that several are badly bruised.

On counting them, he finds that 98 are unsaleable, which is 14% of the total number of apples in the box.

How many apples were in the box?

THINKING LOGICALLY

1.

SNAIL, NINTH, ITCHY, THROW, _____

Does ROBIN, HORSE, TRIBE or CHARM continue the sequence?

2.

3	6	9	4	2	7	■	4	1	6	5	9	8
2	7	8	5	3	6	■	?	?	?	?	?	?

The top set of six numbers has a relationship to the set of six numbers below. The two sets of six boxes on the left have the same relationship as the two sets of six boxes on the right. Which set of numbers should therefore replace the question marks?

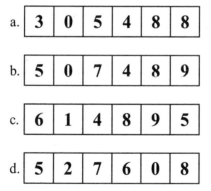

a.	3	0	5	4	8	8

b.	5	0	7	4	8	9

c.	6	1	4	8	9	5

d.	5	2	7	6	0	8

e.	2	1	4	8	9	9

3.

3962 (37)   3895 (63)   7286 (14)   9153 (?)

What number should replace the question mark?

THINKING LOGICALLY

4.

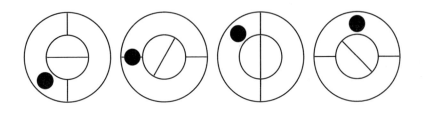

What comes next in the above sequence?

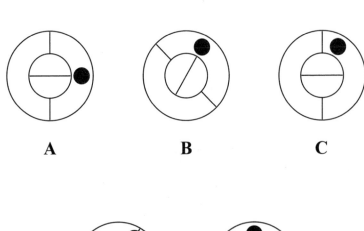

A   **B**   **C**

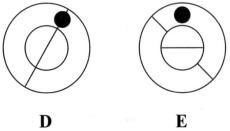

D   **E**

THINKING LATERALLY AND CREATIVELY

1.
What letter is missing?

T N O R F O T ? C A B

2.
What commonality links these words?

BINS, FORT, BOXY, ALMOST, ENVY, DINT, DENT, CRUX

Symbolic Odd One Out Puzzles

1.
Which is the odd one out?

a.　♥ ↑ ▼ § #

b.　♣ ♦ Π ▲ Ψ

c.　# § ▼ ↑ ♥

d.　Ψ Π ♣ ↑ #

e.　# ↑ ♣ Π Ψ

2.

Which is the odd one out?

a. ¥ ® ¢ £ ¶

b. ¢ ¥ ® ¶ £

c. ® ¢ ¥ ¶ £

d. ® ¢ Ψ £ ¶

e. ® ¥ ¶ ¢ £

3.

Which is the odd one out?

a. ← → ↕ ↓ ← ↕ ↔

b. ↕ ↓ ← ↕ ← → ↔

c. ↓ ← ↕ ← → ↔ ↕

d. ← → ↔ ↕ ↓ ← ↕

e. ↕ ← → ↔ ↕ ↓ ←

THINKING SPATIALLY

1.

In the grid below each of the boxes numbered 1A to 3C should contain all the symbols in the box on the top line (boxes 1, 2, 3) and down the side (boxes A, B, C). Thus box 1A should contain all the symbols from boxes 1 and A.

One of the boxes is incorrect. Which one?

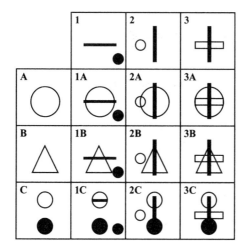

2.

How many lines appear below?

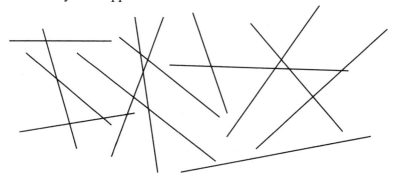

3.

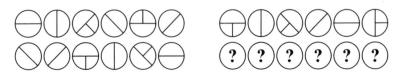

The top set of six circles has a relationship to the set of six circles below. The two sets of six circles on the left have the same relationship as the two sets of six circles on the right.

Which set of circles should, therefore, replace the question marks?

A

B

C

D

E

MEMORY

1.
Study the set of figures below for two minutes, then turn to the next page:

♪ ▲ 3 $ 4 ☼ 8 ♣ 9 ♪ W 3 Ξ

2.
This exercise tests your ability to remember pairs of words and form associations.

BRIEFCASE	MAGPIE	ROSETTE
CAMERA	I-POD	GIRAFFE
MIRROR	HAMBURGER	SKATEBOARD
MOUSE	HAYSTACK	TREE
RIVER	COMPUTER	FROG
CABBAGE	CALENDAR	PUPPY
BUCKET	WINDMILL	SHOE
WALL	DOOR	ORCHESTRA

Study the 12 pairs of words for 10 minutes and use your imagination to link each pair of words, as shown above, in as many ways as possible.

Now turn to the next page.

BRAIN WORKOUT TWO

MEMORY

1.

i) Which symbol appears in the set twice?

ii) Which number appears in the set twice?

When you have an answer, turn back to see if you are correct.

2.

Put a letter A against one pair, the letter B against a second pair etc, through to the letter L until you have matched what you think are the original 12 pairs of words:

MIRROR	SKATEBOARD	MAGPIE
FROG	GIRAFFE	CALENDAR
WINDMILL	HAMBURGER	WALL
ORCHESTRA	CAMERA	PUPPY
HAYSTACK	SHOE	I-POD
TREE	MOUSE	COMPUTER
BRIEFCASE	DOOR	RIVER
BUCKET	ROSETTE	CABBAGE

When you have an answer, turn back to see if you are correct.

Any numerical questions should be solved without the aid of a calculator. (Time Limit 45 minutes)

1.

19, 38, ? , 76, 95, 114

What number should replace the question mark?

2.
Only one group of six letters below can be arranged to spell out a six-letter word in the English language: find the word.

FEMODU   NEVIOC   WPONAB

YIKLAC   TEANGO

3.
Which two circles below are out of sequence?

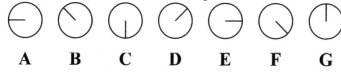

A   B   C   D   E   F   G

4.

42, 96, 3, 21, 17, 11, 23, 69, ?

What number should replace the question mark?

5.
Study the sentence below for one minute then turn straight to the question at the bottom of the next page:

The famous screen comic Charlie Chaplin once entered a Charlie Chaplin look-alike contest, but was unsuccessful.

6.
What pair of rhyming words provide the answer to the clue:
Perfect repast?

7.
A man walks one mile South, then two miles East, then two miles
North, then one mile West and finally one mile South.

How far, and in what direction is he from his original starting
point?

8.
What is 62 multiplied by 7?

9.
If   NEE is to OFF

And   SHEER is to TIFFS

Then   STAR is to ?

10.

DATA, LAMB, EPIC, SOLD, MILE, ?

Which of the following words comes next?

a. TREE   b. LEAF   c. BARK   d. TWIG

Question:
How many times does the letter C appear in the sentence?

THINKING QUICKLY

Find the Missing Symbol Exercise. Target time three minutes per question:

1.

The sequence above consists of a repeated series of symbols. You have to work out what repeated sequence is occurring and from this determine, from the choice below, not only which symbol is missing but from where within the sequence it has been omitted.

    a. ♣

    b. 𝔽

    c. ▶

    d. ♪

2.

The sequence above consists of a repeated series of symbols. You have to work out what repeated sequence is occurring and from this determine, from the choice below, not only which symbol is missing but from where within the sequence it has been omitted.

    a. ⌐|

    b. ╪

    c. ⫠

    d. ⌐⌐

Find the Letter Exercise. Target time 15 minutes:

| A | B | C | D | E | F | G | H |

1.
Which letter is immediately to the left of the letter which is four places to the right of the letter C?

2.
Which letter is immediately to the right of the letter which is three places to the left of the letter which is immediately to the left of the letter which is two places to the right of the letter C?

3.
Which letter comes midway between the letter immediately to the right of the letter A and the letter which is three places to the right of the letter C?

4.
Which letter is two places to the right of the letter which is immediately to the right of the letter which is two places to the left of the letter G?

5.
Which letter is four places to the left of the letter which is two places to the right of the letter which is immediately to the left of the letter which is two places to the right of the letter D?

THINKING VERBALLY

1.

What letter makes a small animal weak and feeble?

2.

Which pair of rhyming words provide the answer to the clue:
Yesteryear whodunnit?

3.

What four letter word follows the following to create six new
words?

TH ____

D ____

T ____

F ____

G ____

SH ____

4.

Select two words that are synonyms, plus an antonym of these two
synonyms, from the list of words below:

**LATE, SLAPDASH, PERFUNCTORY,
ACCIDENTAL, PUNCTILIOUS, HILARIOUS**

5.
Use every word of the phrase GOT ABOUT AGAIN once each only to spell out the name of two islands in the Caribbean.

6.
DID TRUCE is an anagram of two 'this and that' words CUT, DRIED (cut and dried). STAB DARK BEEF is an anagram of which two other 'this and that' words?

7.
What is the longest word in the English language that can be produced from these letters:

N A U R P L I M C E

No letter may be used more than once.

8.
Only one group of six letters below can be arranged to spell out a six-letter word in the English language. Find the word.

MEHLAK

DINURY

MEOPLC

AGLILT

ATPOBG

EVOLNT

THINKING NUMERICALLY

1.

Insert the numbers listed into the circles so that for any particular circle the sum of the numbers in the circles connected to it equals the value corresponding to that circled number in the list. For example:

1 = 14 (4 + 7 + 3)
3 = 1
4 = 8 (1 + 7)
7 = 5 (1 + 4)

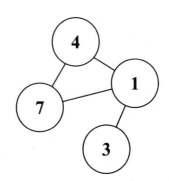

1 = 5
2 = 10
3 = 15
4 = 5
5 = 10
6 = 10

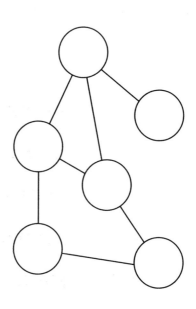

2.
A manufacturing company produces red, white and blue gizmos in the ratio 9 : 4 : 6.

If 1,064 gizmos are produced every hour how many blue gizmos are produced?

3.
The third digit is three more than the first digit, which is double the fourth digit, which is six less than the second digit.

How many four-figure numbers are being described and what are they?

4.
Insert numbers into the remaining blank squares so that the sums in each row and column are correct. All numbers to be inserted are lower than 10.

8	÷		x		=	6
+	■	x	■	−	■	−
	+		+	2	=	
÷	■	÷	■	+	■	+
	x	4	−		=	
=	■	=	■	=	■	=
3	÷		+		=	7

THINKING LOGICALLY

1.

What should replace the question mark?

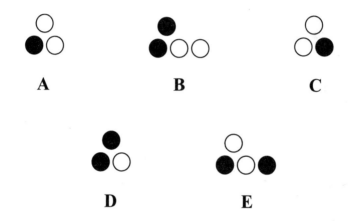

2.
What letter is missing?

A B D ? K P V

3.

4856392 is to **6952843**

as

8734591 is to **?**

THINKING LOGICALLY

4.

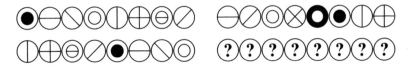

The top set of eight circles has a relationship to the set of eight circles below. The two sets of eight circles on the left have the same relationship as the two sets of eight circles on the right.

Which set of circles should, therefore, replace the question marks?

A

B

C

D

E

THINKING LATERALLY AND CREATIVELY

1.

What number should replace the question mark:

8	6	3	3
3	4	5	5
5	2	6	4
7	7	4	?

2.

What commonality links the words NIMBLE, SOURCE, SWALLOW and NARROW?

3.

In a bowl of fruit, if all but nine are peaches, all but nine are pears, all but nine are plums and all but nine are pineapples, how many pieces of fruit are in the bowl?

4.

SORE	CAT
ALL	WING
LOVE	LAG
DIVE	CUB
CURSE	RAGE

Add a letter (not necessarily the same letter) to each of the words above (at the beginning middle or end) to find ten words all on the same theme.

5.
How many circles appear in the figure below?

THINKING SPATIALLY

1.

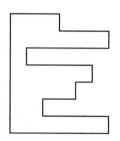

Which piece below, when fitted into the piece above, will form a perfect square?

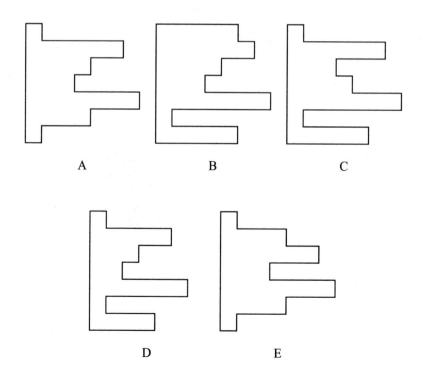

THINKING SPATIALLY

2.

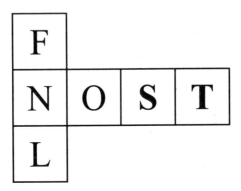

When the above is folded to form a cube, just one of the following can be produced: which?

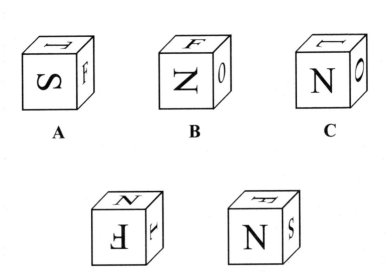

A   B   C

D   E

MEMORY

Study the following, which is an extract from a diary for 12 days in March, for five minutes. Now turn straight to the next page.

Date	Morning	Afternoon	Evening
Monday 10th		Appointment with Optician 3.15pm	
Tuesday 11th	Business appointment with Eileen Dover Construction Company 11.30am		
Wednesday 12th	Phone Rex Holmes		Theatre 6.30pm
Thursday 13th	Sales conference 8.30am		
Friday 14th			
Saturday 15th		Golf (1.30pm tee-off time)	
Sunday 16th	Car Boot Sale 9.00 am		Dinner with Diane and Eric 8.30pm
Monday 17th	Collect Topsy Sharpe from Airport 7.15am		
Tuesday 18th			
Wednesday 19th	Mum and Dad's 45th Wedding Anniversary		
Thursday 20th			
Friday 21st	Take car into garage for servicing 8.30am		

BRAIN WORKOUT THREE
MEMORY

Questions:

    i. The diary covers 12 days during which month?

   ii. Which wedding anniversary will be celebrated on Wednesday 19th?

  iii. What time is Monday's appointment with the optician?

   iv. With whom, on Sunday, is the dinner date?

    v. What appointment is scheduled for Tuesday 11th?

   vi. When is the car due to be taken in for servicing?

  vii. What other event occurs on the same day as the dinner date?

 viii. Who is scheduled to be picked up from the airport on Monday, and at what time?

   ix. What is happening at 1.30 on Saturday?

    x. Who needs to be telephoned on the afternoon of Wednesday 12th?

   xi. What is scheduled for Thursday 13th?

  xii. What is scheduled for the evening of Wednesday 12th?

When you have an answer to all 12 questions, turn back to see if you are correct.

THINKING QUICKLY

1.
Target Time three minutes:

The sequence above consists of a repeated series of symbols. You have to work out what repeated sequence is occurring and from this determine, from the choice below, not only which symbol is missing but from where within the sequence it has been omitted.

a. ▲

b. ●

c. ▼

d. ♀

2.
Target time two minutes:

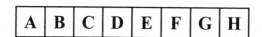

What letter is immediately to the right of the letter which is two places to the left of the letter which is three places to the right of the letter which is immediately to the left of the letter D?

3.
Letter/Code Change Exercise

Code	Function
♫	Exchange the third and fifth letters
Σ	Delete the second letter
&	Add the letter H between the fourth and fifth letters
╫	Reverse the whole sequence
♣	Reverse the last three letters
Ω	Add the letters PC to the end of the sequence

Example: K T B R C N L E → ♣ + & + ╫
Answer: N L E C H R B T K

Explanation:

Stage 1: ♣ Reverse the letters N L E = K T B R C E L N

Stage 2: & Add the letter H between the fourth and fifth letters
K T B R H C E L N

Stage 3: ╫ Reverse the whole sequence N L E C H R B T K

Now try the following five questions (Target time: 10 minutes)

1.
P S T H J U Z L N M → ♫ + ╫ + Ω + &

2.
M Y W P L H G Z T → ♣ + ╫ + & + Σ

3.
H F D A E P L J Y R B → ♫ + ♣ + & + Ω + Σ

4.
G R P J C L E R L T → ╫ + ♫ + & + Σ + Ω + ╫

5.
D F P U T B M S Z X R → & + ♫ + ╫ + Ω + Σ

THINKING VERBALLY

1.

What is the longest word in the English language that can be produced from the ten letters below? No letter may be used more than once.

I C M E O K P N B W

2.

Select two words that are synonyms, plus an antonym of these two synonyms, from the list of words below.

DEARTH, COVENANT, LIFE, PLETHORA, GLUT, ENERGY

3.

If meat in a river (3 in 6) is T(HAM)ES can you find the words and containers for the following?

a.

Feline in a designated place (3 in 8)

b.

Metallic element in the surrounding conditions (4 in 11)

c.

Capital city in an examination of resemblance (5 in 10)

d.

Mode of transportation in a restriction (5 in 10)

e.

Tree in felicity (4 in 9)

4.

Magic Word Square

The answer to each clue is a five-letter word. When the five correct answers are placed into the grid in the correct order they will form a Magic Word Square where the same five words can be read both horizontally and vertically. The clues are in no particular order.

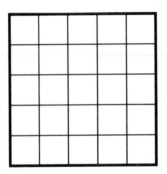

Clues:

Sound reception

Slow moving arboreal mammal

Stacks

The same number

Pigment or colouring substance

THINKING NUMERICALLY

Complete the Equation Exercise

In each of the following choose the number that will correctly complete the equation from the options provided below.

In the first instance try to complete the test in your head without the aid of a calculator or pencil and paper.

Target Time 10 minutes:

1.

| 7 | 9 | 3 | + | ? | 6 | = | 8 | 7 | 9 |

6	5	9	8	7
A	B	C	D	E

2.

| 2 | 3 | 4 | x | 7 | = | 1 | ? | 3 | 8 |

6	4	9	3	5
A	B	C	D	E

3.

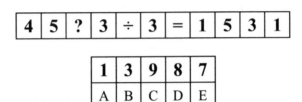

| 4 | 5 | ? | 3 | ÷ | 3 | = | 1 | 5 | 3 | 1 |

1	3	9	8	7
A	B	C	D	E

4.

| 6 | 2 | 8 | + | 5 | 9 | 7 | = | 1 | 2 | ? | 5 |

1	3	8	2	5
A	B	C	D	E

5.

| 7 | 2 | 9 | . | 5 | x | 7 | = | 5 | 1 | ? | 6 | . | 5 |

0	1	2	3	5
A	B	C	D	E

6.

| 2 | 6 | . | 7 | 5 | x | 1 | 3 | = | 3 | 4 | ? | . | 7 | 5 |

5	7	2	0	9
A	B	C	D	E

THINKING LOGICALLY

1.

Which tile should go in the bottom right-hand corner?

A   **B**   **C**   **D**

2.

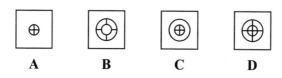

Which two symbols should replace the question marks?

a.

b.

c.

d.

THINKING LOGICALLY

3.

4	9	6	3	7	2		8	6	2	4	1	5
2	7	4	5	9	4		?	?	?	?	?	?

The top set of six numbers has a relationship to the set of six numbers below. The two sets of six boxes on the left have the same relationship as the two sets of six boxes on the right. Which set of numbers should therefore replace the question marks?

a. | 6 | 4 | 0 | 6 | 3 | 7 |
|---|---|---|---|---|---|

b. | 4 | 6 | 0 | 3 | 6 | 7 |
|---|---|---|---|---|---|

c. | 6 | 4 | 1 | 6 | 3 | 6 |
|---|---|---|---|---|---|

d. | 4 | 6 | 0 | 3 | 6 | 8 |
|---|---|---|---|---|---|

e. | 4 | 3 | 1 | 8 | 2 | 10 |
|---|---|---|---|---|---|

THINKING LATERALLY AND CREATIVELY

1.
What number should replace the question mark?

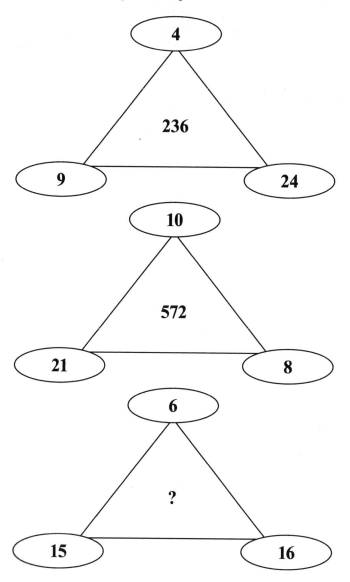

2.
Verbosities

In each of the following a familiar phrase has been disguised by the use of flowery language. Can you work out the three phrases?

For example:
I am making a sound indicative of mirth or pleasure on my entire journey to a place of monetary deposit. What am I doing?

Answer: Laughing all the way to the bank.

i.
I am causing a reaction so lacking in interest as to cause mental weariness to such an extent that I am inducing the removal of a lower garment from the person whom I am addressing. What am I doing?

ii.
Due to an incorrect interpretation of the facts I am erroneously grasping the extremity of a small shoot or branch. What am I doing?

iii.
In order to effect the commencement of a project I am appropriating the outset of the circular propulsion of a spherical projectile. What am I doing?

3.
In which month did I go to Quebec, stay in a hotel, play golf and dance the tango with Juliet?

THINKING SPATIALLY

1.

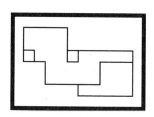

Which two pieces below, when superimposed on each other will produce the figure in the rectangle above?

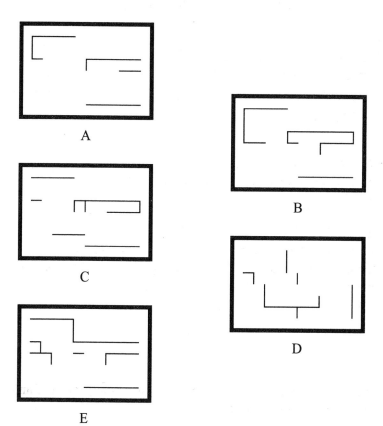

A

B

C

D

E

THINKING SPATIALLY

2.
Which three of the four pieces below can be fitted together to form a perfect circle?

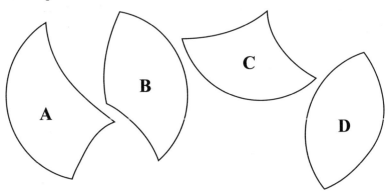

3.
How many squares appear below?

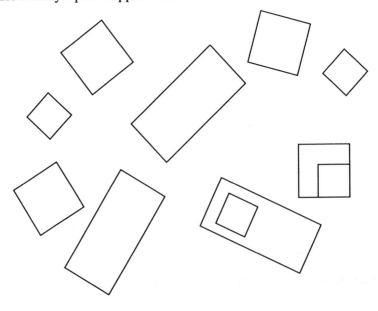

MEMORY

1.

Ξ ‡ ♪ ↑ ☺ ∂ + ♣ ↕

Study the above for two minutes, then turn straight to the next page.

2.
Study the following shopping list for five minutes.

Jar of instant coffee

Frozen oven chips

Raspberry trifle

Cheshire cheese

Tin of garden peas

Packet of waffles

Packet of six pork chops

Packet of brown sugar

Jar of strawberry jam

Pack of four croissants

Now wait for five minutes and turn to the next page.

BRAIN WORKOUT FOUR
MEMORY

1.

a. Which symbol appears immediately to the right of the ∂?

b. Which set of three symbols appears in the order shown below:

♪ ↑ Ξ   ǂ ♪ ✝   ♪ ↑ ☺   ↑ ☺ ✝   ♣ ↑ ǂ

c.
Which symbol appears between the ✝ and ↕?

When you have an answer to each of the above questions, turn back to see if you are correct.

2.
Write out the ten items on the shopping list. The order is not important.

_____

_____

_____

_____

_____

_____

_____

_____

_____

_____

When you have an answer, turn back to see if you are correct.

Any numerical questions should be solved without the aid of a calculator. (Time Limit 45 minutes)

1.

January, May, July, November, January, ?

Which month comes next?

2.
The clues 'Plunder' and 'Musical instrument' lead to which pair of words that sound alike but are spelled differently?

3.

100, 92.5, 82.5, 70, 55, ?

What number should replace the question mark?

4.

ABNFK   is to   KNBFA

As CTMJP   is to   ?????

5.
Study the list of numbers below for two minutes and then turn straight to the question at the bottom of the next page:

29561086495621639632

6.
Which day of the week is two days before the day after the day three days after the day before Tuesday?

7.

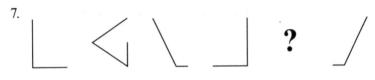

What figure should replace the question mark?

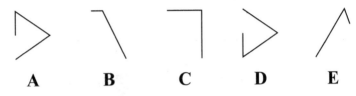

A   **B**   **C**   **D**   **E**

8.
The phrase MERRY DEUCE is an anagram of which two words that are similar in meaning?

9.
It is 13 minutes to the hour on a clock face that shows the time in Roman numerals. Place the following in the order that they appear looking anti-clockwise from the minute hand:

XII   III   VIII   X   V

10.
Tom, Dick and Harriet have £672 between them. The combined amount of money that Tom and Harriet have is twice as much as Dick's. The combined amount of money that Dick and Harriet have is the same as Tom's. How much money has each?

THINKING QUICKLY

Complete the Words Puzzle Exercise. Target time 20 minutes.

1.
Complete the two eight-letter words reading clockwise, which must be similar in meaning. In each word you must find the starting point and provide the two missing letters.

I		O
N	■	L
A	M	

	T	A
A	■	
D	N	U

2.
Complete the two eight-letter words reading clockwise, which must be opposite in meaning. In each word you must find the starting point and provide the two missing letters.

C	U	L
E	■	
L		A

N		O
I	■	
T	N	E

3.

Complete the two eight-letter words reading clockwise, which must be opposite in meaning. In each word you must find the starting point and provide the two missing letters.

N	T	D
E	■	
	I	L

	L	E
R	■	
A	C	S

4.

Complete the two eight-letter words reading clockwise, which must be similar in meaning. In each word you must find the starting point and provide the two missing letters.

O		N
R	■	D
	U	S

N		I
E	■	R
E	L	

THINKING VERBALLY

1.
What is the longest word in the English language that can be produced from the nine letters below? No letter must be used more than once.

N T I P L M E C Y

2.
Change one letter only in each word below to form a familiar phrase.

TIE   FOX   RAT

3.
Insert the name of an animal onto the bottom row to complete seven three-letter words reading downwards:

N	R	A	R	P	J	L
I	U	G	I	E	A	A

4.
DID TRUCE is an anagram of two 'this and that' words CUT, DRIED (cut and dried). FIRE QUASAR is an anagram of which two other this and that words?

5.

Complete the six words below so that the same two letters that finish the first word also start the second word and the same two letters that finish the second word also start the third word etc. The two letters that complete the sixth word also start the first word, to complete the circle.

```
*   *   G   A   *   *

*   *   M   B   *   *

*   *   L   U   *   *

*   *   T   A   *   *

*   *   C   O   *   *

*   *   D   D   *   *
```

6.

Clueless Crossword

In each box which contains four letters, delete three of these letters to produce a crossword containing good English words across and down.

SE TH	I	TL NP	EF AC	PO SE	R	AE RN
N	■	A	■	KU VA	■	RW ON
IO AE	N	AU ID	GO MS	AE IO	T	AX EL
OR TC	■	HC VU	■	D	■	C
EL IM	L	ET RB	M	AE YK	WL ND	ET FC

THINKING NUMERICALLY

1.
Multiplication Exercise

Complete the table by multiplying the numbers along the top by the numbers down the side. For example: referring to the number already inserted; 5 x 7 = 35.

Try to complete the exercise in your head without the use of a calculator or pencil and paper.

Target time 20 minutes:

x	3	9	7	12	8
6					
13					
5			35		
11					
12					
8					
14					
25					

2.
How old is Samantha if in two years time she will be twice as old as she was five years ago?

3.
The cost of a three-course lunch is £21.00.

The main course costs twice as much as the dessert and the dessert costs twice as much as the starter.

How much does each course cost?

4.

0, 1, 3, 4, 6, 9, 9, 16, 12, ?, ?

What two numbers continue the sequence?

5.

11	1	24	10	15
17	7	25	9	28
2	5	6	8	14
68	4	27	12	13
32	37	3	20	16

Looking at straight rows horizontally, vertically and diagonally, what number is two places away from itself plus 5, three places away from itself multiplied by 4, two places away from itself less 3 and three places away from itself plus 9?

THINKING LOGICALLY

Number Logic Grid Puzzles Exercise

In each of the following five puzzles, each set of nine numbers relate to each other in a certain way. Work out the logic behind the numbers in the left-hand box in order to determine which number is missing from the right-hand box. Target Time: 20 minutes

1.

2	4	6		1	3	5
3	6	9		2	5	8
1	5	9		?	4	8

2.

3	2	7		9	2	7
8	4	0		4	6	8
1	6	5		5	?	3

3.

8	1	2		7	6	9
5	8	3		5	9	7
2	2	9		1	?	2

THINKING LOGICALLY

4.

1	3	5		2	5	?
9	8	7		8	9	8
6	1	7		7	6	3

5.

5	2	6		3	1	3
3	7	9		6	4	9
6	2	7		1	?	7

THINKING LATERALLY AND CREATIVELY

1.

3	2	4	1
7	9	5	11
8	9	5	12
2	2	4	?

What number should replace the question mark?

2.
Which two words are the odd ones out:

ODE   POODLE   ICE   TRYING
OLD   NEARER   MISCUE   HOWLED
ACT   ERR   MOHAIR   RIG

3.

Which tile should replace the question mark?

A   **B**   **C**   **D**

4.

Which is the odd one out?

a.   ♀ ♪ → ☺ ← — ◀

b.   — ◀ ♀ ♪ → ☺ ←

c.   ♪ ← ☺ → — ◀ ♀

d.   ◀ ♀ ♪ → ☺ ← —

5.

Which is the odd one out?

a.   ↕ Ψ ® ☺ ♫ ‡ £ ♣

b.   ‡ ♣ £ ↕ Ψ ® ☺ ♫

c.   ↕ £ ‡ ♣ Ψ ☺ ® ♫

d.   ‡ ♫ ☺ ® ♀ ♣ ↕ £

e.   Ψ ♣ ↕ £ ☺ ® ♫ ‡

THINKING SPATIALLY

1.

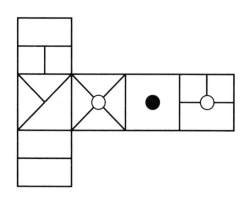

When the above is folded to form a cube, just one of the following can be produced: which?

A

B

C

D

E

THINKING SPATIALLY

2.
Which is the odd one out?

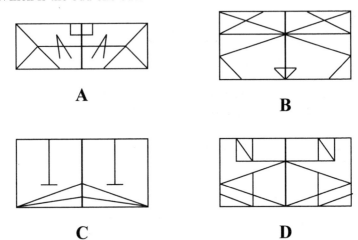

A

B

C

D

3.
How many circles appear below?

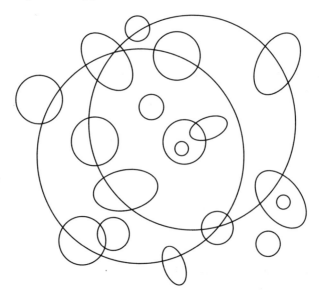

MEMORY

1.

This exercise tests your ability to remember people's names and form associations.

JAMES	HAZEL	ALICE
TONY	ROBERT	JOAN
DAVID	ANGELA	MARION
JEAN	PETER	KEITH
DAN	SUSAN	MATTHEW
MELISSA	EMILY	RUTH

Study the nine pairs of names for three minutes and use your imagination to link each pair of names, as shown above.

Now turn to the next page.

2.

Try to memorise the rows of figures in five minutes then turn straight to the next page.

3   6   2   4   7   1   9

8   3   2   5   9   3   6

5   2   8   3   0   6   7

MEMORY

1.
Put a letter A against one pair, the letter B against a second pair
etc, through to the letter I until you have matched what you think
are the original nine pairs of names:

ANGELA	ALICE	KEITH
JEAN	MELISSA	MATTHEW
JAMES	ROBERT	PETER
JOAN	EMILY	DAN
RUTH	HAZEL	DAVID
MARION	TONY	SUSAN

When you have an answer, turn back to see if you are correct.

2.
a.
What are the first two digits on the top row?
b.
In which row does the zero appear?
c.
What is the final number on the bottom row?
d.
Which is the only number to appear twice on the same row?
e.
What number appears in the same position in both the first and
second rows?
f.
How many times does the number one appear?

When you have answers to all of the above, turn back to see if you
are correct.

THINKING QUICKLY

1.

Letter and Number Arrangement Exercise

Arrange the numbers in ascending order followed by the letters in reverse alphabetical order. Target Time 10 minutes.

i.

T 4 L K N E 6 C 9 2 M D

_____

ii.

D T 5 S M 7 F J Z P 9 3 6

_____

iii.

9 F 3 A N H T C Q X 5 7 U 8 D

_____

iv.

U 6 4 G X S A J L 8 F W Q 5 2 B

_____

v.

U B Q L 8 J Y 5 2 X P K G T 6 S E

_____

2.
Fives (Target Time 20 minutes)

Insert the five-letter words in the grid to complete the crossword.

YODEL	TEACH	UPPER	ALLOT	EXCEL	EDICT
SABOT	OVATE	SHELF	LITHE	SHYLY	ENSUE
PSALM	ENTRY	OTHER	TUTTI	URBAN	ATLAS
ENACT	LILAC	INDEX	CHUTE	PROBE	NEEDY
PREEN	THUMB	SPOUT	ENNUI	TOAST	YIELD
FILED	TASTY	HOTLY	ENDUE	ISSUE	EXULT

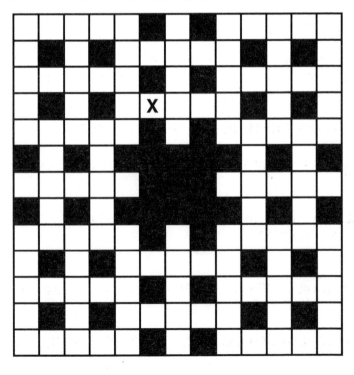

THINKING VERBALLY

1.

Insert two letters into each pair of brackets so that they finish the word on the left and start the word on the right. The letters in the brackets, reading in pairs downwards, will spell out an eight-letter word.

PL (* *) EW

WH (* *) OM

AC (* *) AT

PU (* *) RK

2.
Theme Puzzles

In the three puzzles below a number of words are listed on the same theme. Try to find another word on the same theme by taking one letter from each word in turn.

For example: GRAPE, PEACH, ORANGE, CHERRY

Answer: PEAR (GRAPE, PEACH, ORANGE, CHERRY)

i.
PELICAN, GOSHAWK, HERON, SWAN, OSTRICH, EAGLE, CRANE, TOUCAN

ii.
CAPRICORN, GEMINI, TAURUS, CANCER, LEO, ARIES

iii.
BLOUSE, UNDERWEAR, TIE, HAT, COAT, JACKET, SHIRT

3.
Noughts and Crosswords

I	A	N
T	L	E
O	R	P

In this puzzle there are eight answers to find. The clues are in matching pairs, the answer to each clue uses three letters in a line one way round and the other clue uses the same letters in reverse order. The letters appear consecutive in the middle of the word you are seeking.

For example: Letters OTI and ITO
Clues: Strikingly strange and unusual (Answer: EXOTIC)
         Leader writer (Answer: EDITOR)

i.
Letters ALR and RLA
Clues: Medieval principles of knighthood
         Crown with flowers or branches
ii.
Letters NEP and PEN
Clues: Incompetent and ineffectual
         Woodworker
iii.
Letters PLI and ILP
Clues: Elevate
         An engineless plane
iv.
Letters IAN and NAI
Clues: Gargantuan
         Gastropod mollusc

THINKING NUMERICALLY

1.
Insert numbers into the remaining blank squares so that the sums in each row and column are correct. All numbers to be inserted are lower than 10.

	+		÷	4	=	3
−	■	−	■	+	■	−
	x		÷	6	=	
x	■	+	■	÷	■	+
2	÷		+	5	=	
=	■	=	■	=	■	=
4	+		−		=	

2.

10, 10.5, 9.75, 10.75, 9.5, ?

What number should replace the question mark?

3.
How many cases do you need if you have to pack 238 pairs of shoes into cases that each hold 34 shoes?

4.
How many minutes is it before 12 noon if 18 minutes ago it was twice as many minutes past 10.00am?

5.

Insert the numbers 1 – 6 into the circles so that:

The numbers 4 and 6 and all the numbers between total 21
The numbers 6 and 5 and all the numbers between total 15
The numbers 3 and 2 and all the numbers between total 11

6.
Phil has £150 and three-quarters of what Jill has, and Jill has £100
and half of what Phil has, so how much have each?

THINKING LOGICALLY

1.

647(17), 373 (18), 486 (26), 999 (?)

What number should replace the question mark?

2.
What number follows 616, 617, 627, 727, 728, 738?

3.
An electrical circuit wiring a set of four lights depends on a system of switches A, B, C and D. Each switch when working has the following effect on the lights:

Switch A turns lights 1 and 2 on/off or off/on
Switch B turns lights 2 and 4 on/off or off/on
Switch C turns lights 1 and 3 on/off or off/on
Switch D turns lights 3 and 4 on/off or off/on

⭕ = ON   ⚫ = OFF

In the following, switches D, C, B and A are thrown in turn, with the result that Set 1 is transformed into Set 2. One of the switches is not, therefore, working and has had no effect on the numbered lights. Identify which one of the switches is not working.

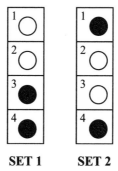

SET 1   SET 2

THINKING LOGICALLY

4.

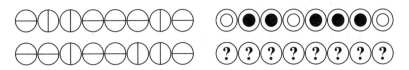

The top set of eight circles has a relationship to the set of eight circles below. The two sets of eight circles on the left have the same relationship as the two sets of eight circles on the right.

Which set of circles should, therefore, replace the question marks?

A

B

C

D

E

THINKING LATERALLY AND CREATIVELY

1.
Which is the odd one out?

84326   742816   63188   521646   785630

2.

A	B	O
C	U	?
A	T	E

What letter should replace the question mark?

3.
A frugal man collected cigarette ends until he had 1,728. How many cigarettes in total could he make and smoke from these if 12 cigarette ends make up one cigarette.

4.

3	9	7	6
1	2	1	3
8	5	9	9
1	3	1	?

What number should replace the question mark?

5.

What number should replace the question mark?

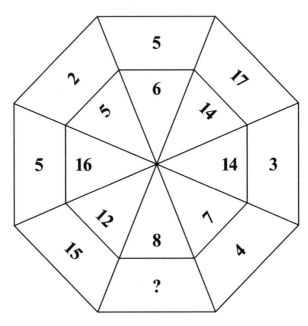

THINKING SPATIALLY

1.

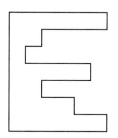

Which piece below, when fitted into the piece above, will form a perfect square?

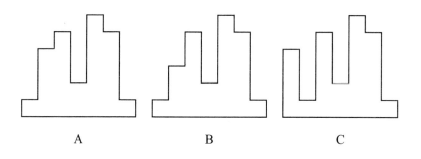

A   B   C

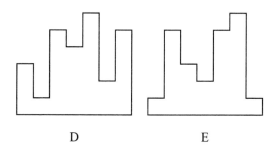

D   E

THINKING SPATIALLY

2.

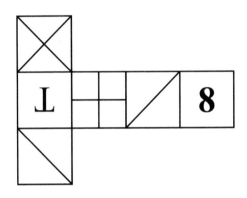

When the above is folded to form a cube, just one of the following can be produced: which?

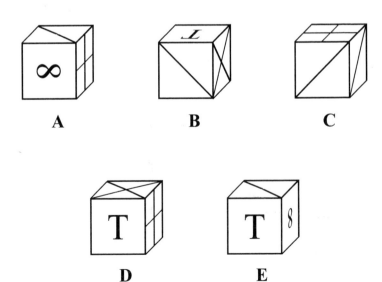

A B C

D E

MEMORY

1.
Study the row of figures below for two minutes.

$$\text{♪ £ § ® ¶ Ω ☺ ∏ + ? ╪}$$

Now wait for one minute, then turn to the next page.

2.
Study these names and professions for five minutes:

Jane Shepherd	**Entertainer**
Maurice Painter	**Joiner**
Tony Cook	**Chauffeur**
Michelle Kitchen	**Tailor**
Karen Naylor	**Baker**
Paul Driver	**Cook**
Amy Singer	**Farmer**

Now turn to the next page.

BRAIN WORKOUT SIX

MEMORY

1.

Which group of three figures below appear adjacent to each other, and in the same order, in the list you looked at one minute ago?

a. ® ¶ £

b. + ? ♪

c. ¶ Ω ‡

d. ∏ + ?

e. § ® Ω

When you have an answer, turn back to see if you are correct.

2.

Complete the remainder of the table with the surnames and professions correctly inserted.

A. Naylor, Singer, Painter, Cook, Driver, Kitchen, Shepherd

B. Farmer, Entertainer, Tailor, Baker, Chauffeur, Cook, Joiner

First name	Surname A	Profession B
Jane	Shepherd	
Maurice		Joiner
Tony	Cook	
Michelle		Tailor
Karen		
Paul		Cook
Amy	Singer	

When you have an answer, turn back to see if you are correct.

Any numerical questions should be solved without the aid of a calculator. (Time Limit 45 minutes)

1.
Which is the odd one out?

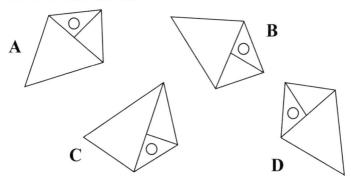

2.

X 2 L F G 6 9 K Y 4 B M N 3

Arrange the odd numbers is ascending order, followed by the letters in reverse alphabetical order, followed by the even numbers in descending order.

3.

Study the above list of card suits for two minutes, then turn straight to the bottom of the next page.

4.

O * * * A * L E   *** A * R * E ***

Complete the two words which are synonyms of the word OBSTRUCTION.

5.

What letter should replace the question mark?

A	D	F	J
C	F	H	L
F	I	K	O
J	M	O	?

6.

PASS, WAY, CAR, HOPE, PORT, WARD, PET, ?

Which four-letter word completes the sequence?

7.

Select two words that are synonyms, plus an antonym of these two synonyms, from the list of words below.

STRICT   DUBIOUS   BINDING
OPTIONAL   WILLING   OBLIGATORY

8.

100, 95, 88, 83, 76, ?

What number should replace the question mark?

9.

Which is the odd one out?

a. ⊦⊦⊓⊣⊣   b. ⊤⊦⊦⊦⊔⊔⊔⊦⊦⊣⊤   c. ⊔⊦⊔⊣⊣⊓⊦⊔⊔⊣⊦   d. ⊦⊦⊦⊣⊣⊓

10.

How tall is a sapling that is three metres shorter than a fence that is four times higher than the sapling?

Question:
Which suit appears most in the list?

THINKING QUICKLY

Find the Missing Symbol Exercise. Target time three minutes per question:

1.

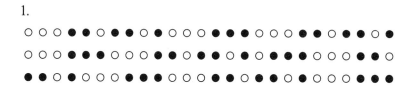

The sequence above consists of a repeated series of symbols. You have to work out what repeated sequence is occurring and from this determine, from the choice below, not only which two symbols are missing but from where within the sequence they have been omitted.

a. ○●   b. ●○   c. ●●   d. ○○

2.

The sequence above consists of a repeated series of symbols. You have to work out what repeated sequence is occurring and from this determine, from the choice below, not only which symbol is missing but from where within the sequence it has been omitted.

a. ☺   b. 〓

c. ♫   d. 〓

Find the Letter Exercise. Target time 15 minutes:

A	B	C	D	E	
F	G	H	I	J	
K	L	M	N	O	
P	Q	R	S	T	
U	V	W	X	Y	Z

1.
Which letter is two places below the letter immediately to the left of the letter which is three places above the letter R?

2.
Which letter is three places to the right of the letter which is immediately below the letter which is two places to the left of the letter which is two below the letter I?

3.
Which letter is immediately to the right of the letter that comes midway between the letter which is two places to the left of the letter W and the letter two places below the letter A?

4.
Which letter is three places to the right of the letter which is two places above the letter which is two places to the left of the letter which is immediately above the letter X?

5.
Which letter is immediately to the right of the letter which is two places below the letter which is three places to the right of the letter which is two places below the letter immediately to the right of the letter A?

THINKING VERBALLY

1.
Which of the following is not an anagram of a river?

SUPERHEAT

AT BINGO

BENAUD

GONK ME

NERVES

NAG ARIA

2.
Each clue leads to a pair of rhyming words, for example:
Sensible Scandinavian = Sane Dane.

a. Guileful deception

b. Laconic profanity

c. Naked puritan

d. Approve Scandinavian

3.

This puzzle consists of five interlocked 4 x 4 Magic Word Squares. Clues are given in groups of four (but in no particular order within each group), and the answer to each is a four-letter word. When placed in their respective grids correctly the four words will form Magic Word Squares where each word can be read both horizontally and vertically.

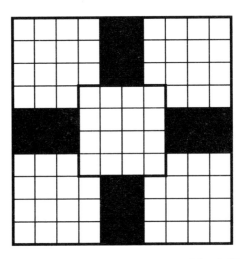

North West Grid
Form of verse
A fit of shivering
Therefore
Bound

South West Grid
Gamble
Remove
Two-wheeled
   vehicle
Song for solo voice

Centre Grid
Notion
Thin Fog
Stratum of coal
Make Gentle

North East Grid
Fit and competent
Former time
Disparage
Limited period
   of time

South East Grid
Apiece
Take regard of
Hint
Shaft on which a
   wheel rotates

THINKING NUMERICALLY

1.

Insert the numbers listed into the circles so that for any particular circle the sum of the numbers in the circles connected to it equals the value corresponding to that circled number in the list. For example:

1 = 14 (4 + 7 + 3)
3 = 1
4 = 8 (1 + 7)
7 = 5 (1 + 4)

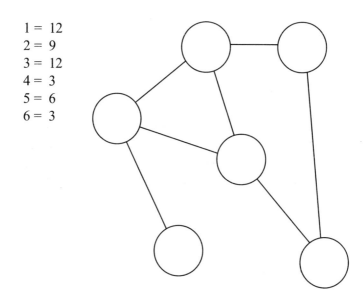

1 = 12
2 = 9
3 = 12
4 = 3
5 = 6
6 = 3

2.

3, 10, 31, 94, ?

What comes next?

3.
I have collected 119 strawberries from my garden which I wish to put into punnets for handing out to my neighbours. I wish each punnet to contain the same number of strawberries and I wish to use the smallest number of punnets possible. How many neighbours received a punnet and how many strawberries did each punnet contain?

4.
In five years' time the combined age of my sister's four children will be 54. What will it be in three years' time?

5.
Jane is twice as old as Cain was when Jane was as old as Cain is now. The combined age of Jane and Cain is 56. How old are Jane and Cain now?

6.
Jim, Alf and Sid share out a certain amount of money between them. Jim gets two fifths, Alf gets 20% and Sid gets £56. How much is the original amount of money?

THINKING LOGICALLY

1.

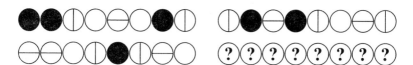

The top set of eight circles has a relationship to the set of eight circles below. The two sets of eight circles on the left have the same relationship as the two sets of eight circles on the right.

Which set of circles should, therefore, replace the question marks?

A

B

C

D

E

2.

2829 (23), 2765 (79), 8238 (?)

What number should replace the question mark?

3.

1, 4, 18, ?, 431, 2150, 10744

What number is missing from the above sequence?

4.

2	8	9	6	4	3	■	4	8	2	9	3	7
5	7	9	2	8	6	■	?	?	?	?	?	?

The top set of six numbers has a relationship to the set of six numbers below. The two sets of six boxes on the left have the same relationship as the two sets of six boxes on the right. Which set of numbers should therefore replace the question marks?

a. | 8 | 6 | 5 | 8 | 7 | 4 |
|---|---|---|---|---|---|

b. | 9 | 8 | 5 | 6 | 9 | 6 |
|---|---|---|---|---|---|

c. | 8 | 8 | 6 | 6 | 9 | 4 |
|---|---|---|---|---|---|

d. | 6 | 9 | 3 | 7 | 4 | 8 |
|---|---|---|---|---|---|

e. | 9 | 6 | 5 | 8 | 7 | 4 |
|---|---|---|---|---|---|

THINKING LATERALLY AND CREATIVELY

1.
What commonality links the words PAINS, SPRUCY, PENAL, RAIN, CHAIN and LAITY?

2.

5901 (13), 6217 (2), 3497 (9), 2831 (?)

What number should replace the question mark?

3.

3	6	1	8
9	4	4	7
6	8	3	4
5	2	2	?

What number should replace the question mark?

4.

Draw the four missing symbols in the grid below in accordance with the rules of logic already established.

⊤	‖	⊢	⊣	⊥⊤
⊣			⊤	‖
⊢			‖	⊤
F	⊢	‖	⊥⊤	⊣
⊥⊤	⊣	⊤	F	⊢

THINKING SPATIALLY

1.

In order to open the safe the nine keys must be pressed in the correct order by following the instructions on each pad, for example: 1S
        2W means move one pad South and two pads West.

It is necessary to find the starting point, then visit every pad, finally finishing at the centre pad *.

1S 1E	1S 1W	1W 2S
2E 1S	*	1S 2W
2N 1E	1E 1N	2N 2W

2.

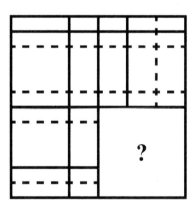

Which tile should go in the bottom right corner?

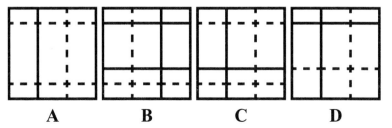

A   B   C   D

THINKING SPATIALLY

3.

In the grid below each of the boxes numbered 1A to 3C should contain all the symbols in the box on the top line (boxes 1, 2, 3) and down the side (boxes A, B, C). Thus box 1A should contain all the symbols from boxes 1 and A.

One of the boxes is incorrect. Which one?

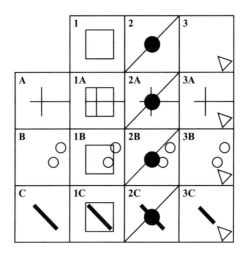

MEMORY

1.
This exercise tests your ability to remember pairs of words and form associations.

PAINTBRUSH	THERMOMETER	CHEESE
CABINET	PAPERCLIP	RABBIT
BOTTLE	GOAT	SHIP
LEVER	KIMONO	DOMINO
SLIPPER	STAR	BATON
CARROT	FOOTBALL	TELEVISION
MOUNTAIN	WILLOW	CIRCLE
LAMP	TARGET	LEAF

Study the 12 pairs of words for 10 minutes and use your imagination to link each pair of words, as shown above, in as many ways as possible.

Now turn to the next page.

2.

Study the above for ten seconds, then wait for five minutes before turning to the next page.

BRAIN WORKOUT SEVEN

MEMORY

1.

Put a letter A against one pair, the letter B against a second pair etc, through to the letter L until you have matched what you think are the original 12 pairs of words:

PAPERCLIP	BOTTLE	GOAT
FOOTBALL	CHEESE	CARROT
KIMONO	SLIPPER	BATON
WILLOW	CABINET	LAMP
CIRCLE	DOMINO	LEAF
TELEVISION	RABBIT	LEVER
PAINTBRUSH	SHIP	STAR
MOUNTAIN	THERMOMETER	TARGET

When you have an answer, turn back to see if you are correct.

2.

Which of the following did you look at five minutes ago?

$	¥
Ψ	%

%	¥
$	Ψ

%	Ÿ
$	¥

%	Ψ
$	¥

$	%
Ψ	¥

When you have an answer, turn back to see if you are correct.

THINKING QUICKLY

1.
Double Letter/Code Change Exercise

Code	Function
♫	Exchange the third letter of the top row with first letter of the bottom row
Σ	Advance the fourth letter of the bottom row by one place in the alphabet
&	Add the letter K between the fourth and fifth letters of the top row
⌗	Reverse the whole of the top row
♣	Reverse the last three letters of the top row
Ω	Exchange the first and last letters of the bottom row

Example: G W P T A L M
           K S R O P T A F → ♣ + ♫ + Σ
Answer: G W K T M L A
           P S R P P T A F

Explanation:

Stage 1: ♣ Reverse the last three letters of the top row
G W P T M L A
K S R O P T A F

Stage 2: ♫ Exchange the third letter of the top row with first letter of the bottom row
G W K T M L A
P S R O P T A F

Stage 3: Σ Advance the fourth letter of the bottom row by one place in the alphabet
G W K T M L A
P S R P P T A F

Now try the following five questions (Target time: 10 minutes)

1.
S P B U R T A K D
A R Y V L X Z O N   →   ‡ + & + ♣

2.
D O B E R M A N N
P I N S C H E R S   →   & + Ω + ♫

3.
H Y P E R B O L I C
P A R A B O L O I D   →   & + ‡ + Σ + ♫

4.
F G O A P M R T Y
Q W E R T Y U I O P   →   Σ + ♣ + ♫ + Ω

5.
J U S T I F I A B L E
E X P E C T A T I O N   →   ‡ + & + ♣ + ♫ + Σ

2.
Two-Word Change Exercise (Target Time five minutes)

Exchange the position of two words only in each of the sentences below so that they then make complete sense:

1.
In human pre-history, the only power augmented was muscle power, available by primitive tools, such as the wedge or lever.

2.
Your computer must be set up as a shared printer on the printer to which it is connected before you access it from another computer.

3.
When there are two main parties, divided along class lines, the one gaining legislation can often undo the power of its predecessor.

THINKING VERBALLY

1.
GAS NETWORK is an anagram of which two words that are opposite in meaning?

2.
Change one letter only in each word to form a familiar phrase:

ANT ODD COW

3.
Find the starting point and work along the connecting lines from letter to letter to spell out a 14-letter word.

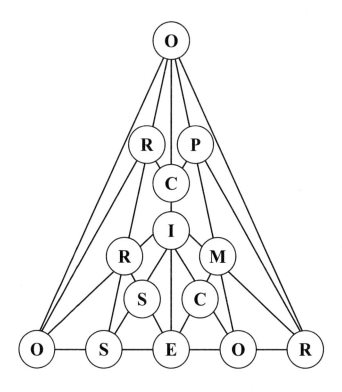

4.
Crossword

Across

1 Wooden shoe (5)

5 Not suitable (5)

7 Bend low (5)

8 Smidgen (4)

10 Facial expression (4)

12 Toxin (5)

14 Savour (5)

15 Time period (5)

Down

1 Concise (8)

2 Bend (3)

3 Matt of grass (4)

4 Subsequently (5)

6 Convey (8)

9 A drink in honour (5)

11 Make level (4)

13 Old horse (3)

THINKING NUMERICALLY

1.

100, 85, 71, 56, 42, ?

What number continues the sequence?

2.
Mary has one and a third times as many as Sid, who has one and a third times as many as Alf, who has one and a third times as many as Jim. Altogether they have 175. How many has each?

3.
Between 12.00 noon and 1.00pm the office received 462 emails, which was 65% more than the number of emails it received between 11.00am and 12.00 noon.

How many emails were received between 11.00am and 12.00 noon?

4.
I travel to work by train and bus. If my train journey takes 29 minutes and my bus journey takes 18 minutes longer, what is my travelling time to work in hours and minutes?

5.
The average of three numbers is 19. The average of two of these numbers is 27. What is the third number?

6.

$$\frac{(3 \times 8) \times 2}{\sqrt{16}} = 3^2 + ?$$

Complete the equation by correctly identifying the missing part of the calculation from the list of options below.

a. **4.5**

b. **3**

c. **2.5**

d. **6**

e. **(3.5 – 1.5)**

7.

In the two numerical sequences below, one number that appears in the top sequence should appear in the bottom sequence and vice versa. Which two numbers should be changed round?

1, 4, 9, 15, 25, 36

3, 5, 9, 16, 23, 33

THINKING LOGICALLY

1.
Which number is the odd one out?

3758   5968   1536   4869   2647

2.

3	1	2	4
4	8	11	17
2	14	33	61
1	17	64	?

What number should replace the question mark?

3.
Draw the contents of the middle tile in accordance with the rules of logic already established.

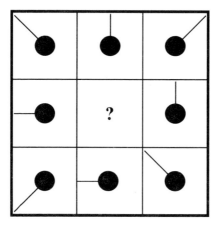

THINKING LOGICALLY

4.

The top set of eight circles has a relationship to the set of eight circles below. The two sets of eight circles on the left have the same relationship as the two sets of eight circles on the right.

Which set of circles should, therefore, replace the question marks?

A

B

C

D

E

THINKING LATERALLY AND CREATIVELY

1.
Which two phrases that are spelled differently but sound alike mean Female feline/Sophisticated headwear?

2.

293   (5448)   624

724   (5684)   347

623   (????)   592

What number should replace the question marks?

3.
Draw one line that will divide the rectangle into two identically shaped sections each containing the same number of circles.

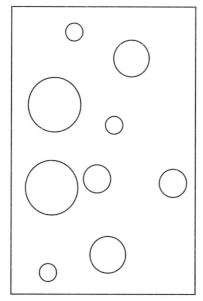

4.

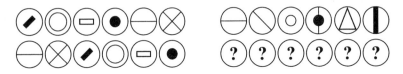

The top set of six circles has a relationship to the set of six circles below. The two sets of six circles on the left have the same relationship as the two sets of six circles on the right.

Which set of circles should, therefore, replace the question marks?

A

B

C

D

E

THINKING SPATIALLY

1.
Which is the odd one out?

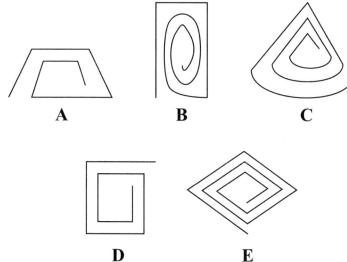

A **B** **C**

D **E**

2.
Which is the odd one out?

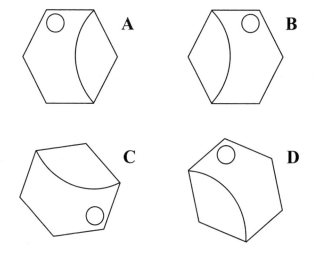

A **B**

C **D**

BRAIN WORKOUT EIGHT

THINKING SPATIALLY

3.
Which of the three pieces below when fitted together will form a perfect square?

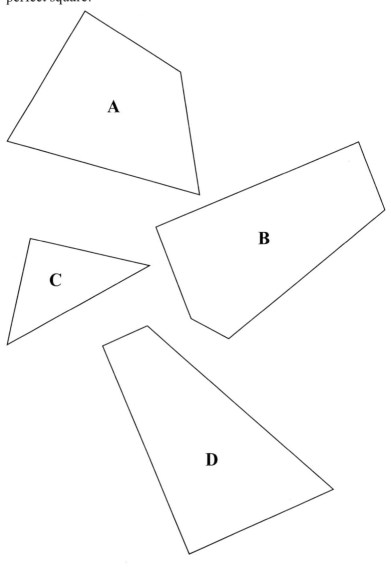

MEMORY

1.

Study the above for 20 seconds, then turn to the next page.

2.

S	T	A	T	E
T	U	T	O	R
A	T	O	N	E
T	O	N	I	C
E	R	E	C	T

Study the above grid for two minutes, then wait for one minute before turning to the next page.

BRAIN WORKOUT EIGHT

MEMORY

1.

Which of the following have you just looked at?

When you have an answer, turn back to see if you are correct.

2.

Complete the grid with the aid of the letters already inserted.

When you have an answer, turn back to see if you are correct.

Any numerical questions should be solved without the aid of a calculator. (Time Limit 45 minutes)

1.
Arrange the letters TWBKFZNOGVYJ in alphabetical order.
What is the longest word in the English language that appears?

2.

╫Ω♣Ξ♫∏╫Ω♣Ξ♫∏╫Ω♣♫∏╫Ω♣Ξ♫∏

Which symbol is missing from the above list and where should it appear?

 a. ╫   b. Ω   c. Ξ   d. ∏

3.

            ?

What comes next?

A   B   C   D   E

4.
What is 588 divided by 14?

5.
Study the list of words for 30 seconds and then turn to the bottom of the next page.

CAT, RAT, OAT, MAT, VAT, FAT,
PAT, BAT, HAT, MAT, SAT, EAT

6.
Which number is the odd one out?

362   416   623   813   281   254   353

7.
COPY   **POLE**

What word links the two words above with the two words below?

NAP   **CALL**

8.
A   E   H   J   N   ?

What letter should replace the question mark?

9.
**TRAIN, NORTH,   ? , YOUNG, GLEAM,
MARCH, HAPPY, YOURS, SABLE, ENJOY**

What word is missing?

a. HOUSE   b. MONEY   c. HONEY   d. MOUSE

10.
3, 6, 10, 15, 21, ?

What comes next?

Question:
Which word appears twice in the list?

THINKING QUICKLY

1.
Anagrammed Synonym Test (Target Time 30 minutes)

In each of the five puzzles below find two of the three words that can be paired to form an anagram that is a synonym of the remaining word. For example, with LEG - MEEK - NET, the words LEG and NET form an anagram of GENTLE, which is a synonym of the remaining word, MEEK.

a. DUBIOUS – ELOQUENT – BIAS

b. RARE – TRAIT – CATCH

c. RENT – CONTEST - AMOUNT

d. ROOT – ASSIST - PEACE

e. TUNE – BELOW – HARDEN

2.
Word/Symbol Speed Exercise

In each question find the longest word that is spelled out by substituting letters for symbols in accordance with the key below.

♫	Ω	£	♣	♂	Σ	∏	⌗	&	#	▲	¶
H	O	Y	P	E	C	W	L	A	T	N	I

Example:

♣	♂	#	Σ	&	▲	¶	▲	♂	#	¶	♂

Answer: CANINE
The words PET, CAN, NINE, NET and TIE also appear, but
CANINE is the longest word that appears in the grid below.

♣	♂	#	Σ	&	▲	¶	▲	♂	#	¶	♂
P	E	T	C	A	N	I	N	E	T	I	E

Target time eight minutes:

1.

#	¶	▲	Σ	╬	Ω	Π	▲	♣	Ω	♂	#

2.

&	Σ	Ω	♣	£	#	¶	Σ	¶	╬	£	♂

3.

#	Ω	♣	&	▲	¶	Σ	Ω	▲	╬	£	#

4.

♣	¶	▲	Σ	♫	&	♣	╬	&	¶	▲	#

5.

♂	Σ	Ω	Π	╬	♂	#	╬	&	Σ	♂	▲

THINKING VERBALLY

1.
Fight and Play

In each of the following find a well-known two word phrase that rhymes with the two words provided. For example: Fight and Play, Answer: Night and Day

a. Handcuff and Grumble

b. Accost and Surround

c. Shock and Cajole

d. Such and Show

e. Pry and Expand

f. Adaptor and Nurse

g. Clamour and Sarongs

h. Overcast and Luxurious

i. Tonight and Surly

j. Allegros and Bonbons

2.
Select two words that are synonyms, plus an antonym of these two synonyms, from the list of words below:

PRIMARY   PRINCIPAL   GRAND,
PARAMOUNT   DOCTRINE   AUXILIARY

3.
Scramblegram

Four 11-letter words all on the theme of the weather have been jumbled. Solve the four anagrams and enter the answers next to each anagram, reading from left to right or top to bottom.

Next transfer the letters in the shaded squares to the keyword box below to find a fifth word (of nine letters) on the same theme.

CYNICALTONE

D E P A R T L U N C H

U P R A T E M E T R E

GOOEYORMELT

KEYWORD

THINKING NUMERICALLY

1.

Insert the numbers listed into the circles so that for any particular circle the sum of the numbers in the circles connected to it equals the value corresponding to that circled number in the list. For example:

1 = 14 (4 + 7 + 3)
3 = 1
4 = 8 (1 + 7)
7 = 5 (1 + 4)

1 = 13
2 = 10
3 = 5
4 = 8
5 = 6
6 = 5

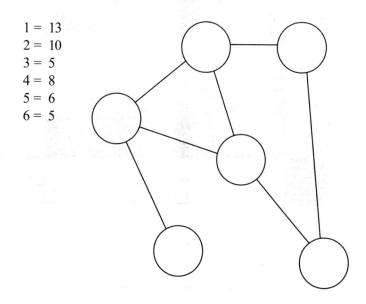

2.

100, 91, 73, 46, ?

What number should replace the question mark to continue the sequence?

3.

4	6		7	5		9	4
2	8		3	8		?	7

What number should replace the question mark?

4.
How many minutes is it before noon if 22 minutes ago it was as many minutes past 10.00am?

5.

482 (34)   697 (61)   732 (??)

What number should replace the question marks?

THINKING LOGICALLY

1.

29, 18, 47, 28, 75, ?, ?

What two numbers come next?

2.

• ↔ → ← ↕ ↕ → • ↕ → ← ↕ ↕ → • ↕ ↓ ← ↕ ↕
→ • ↕ ↓ ↑ ↕ ↕ → • ↕ ↑ ↔ ↕ → • ↕ ↓ ↑ ↔

Which two symbols come next: a. ↕→, b. ↔↓, c. ↕↓, d. ↔→?

3.

5	8	7	3	9	6	█	8	9	6	5	7	8
1	3	1	0	1	5	█	?	?	?	?	?	?

The top set of six numbers has a relationship to the set of six numbers below. The two sets of six boxes on the left have the same relationship as the two sets of six boxes on the right. Which set of numbers should therefore replace the question marks?

a.	1	1	7	1	1	5
b.	1	7	1	2	1	2
c.	1	7	1	1	1	5
d.	2	2	9	1	4	1
e.	7	1	0	1	5	1

THINKING LOGICALLY

4.

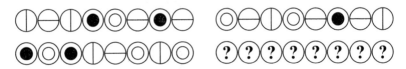

The top set of eight circles has a relationship to the set of eight circles below. The two sets of eight circles on the left have the same relationship as the two sets of eight circles on the right.

Which set of circles should, therefore, replace the question marks?

A

B

C

D

E

THINKING LATERALLY AND CREATIVELY

1.
Add six lines to make sense of the sequence:

2.

3926, 324, 24, ?

What number should replace the question mark?

3.
Draw the contents of the middle tile in accordance with the rules of logic already established.

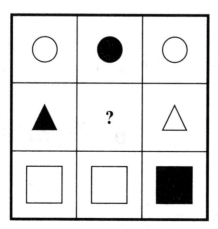

4.

1					1
	3	2		3	
2			3		2
	3			4	
2		?	3		2
	2			2	

What number should replace the question mark?

5.
The name of which Shakespeare character is indicated below:

H : O

THINKING SPATIALLY

1.

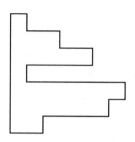

Which piece below, when fitted into the piece above, will form a perfect square?

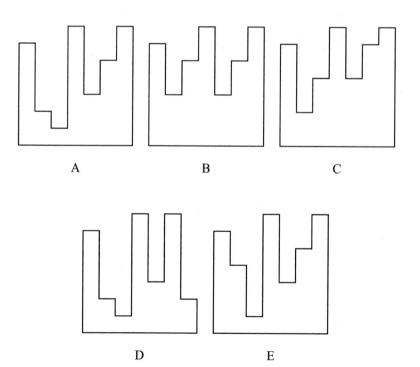

A   B   C

D   E

THINKING SPATIALLY

2.

How many more discs of exactly the same size as the one already placed are needed to completely cover the square?

3.

Which three of the five pieces below when fitted together will form a perfect circle?

A

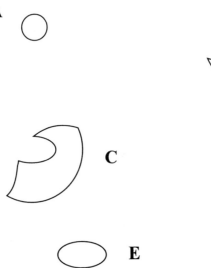

B

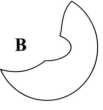

C

D

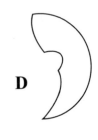

E

MEMORY

1.

Study the above for 10 seconds, then wait for one minute before turning to the next page.

2.

Study the array of numbers for three minutes then turn straight to the next page.

4	9	7	2	6	5
4	2	6	2	7	3
6	5	9	3	3	7
8	6	9	2	5	4

MEMORY

1.

Which of the following did you look at one minute ago?

↑	↑		←	↑		↓	↑		←	↑		↑	↓
←	↑		←	↓		←	↑		↑	↓		→	↑

When you have an answer, turn back to see if you are correct.

2.

i) Which is the only number that appears in every line looking across?

ii) Which number appears three times looking down the fourth column?

iii) Which number appears twice looking down the third column?

iv) Which number appears in both the top left-hand corner and bottom right-hand corner?

v) Which is the only digit from 1-9 that does not appear anywhere in the array?

When you have an answer to each question, turn back to see if you are correct.

THINKING QUICKLY

Anagrammed Synonyms and Antonyms Exercise
(Target Time 20 minutes)

1.
RECTIFY AT TEST is an anagram of which two words that are
similar in meaning?
2.
DUNCE CODED CLUE is an anagram of which two words that
are similar in meaning?
3.
GRAINS OF TURNIP is an anagram of which two words that are
opposite in meaning?
4.
WOMEN USE FUR is an anagram of which two words that are
opposite in meaning?

Double Letter/Code Change Exercise

Code	Function
♫	Exchange the third letter of the top row with first letter of the bottom row
Σ	Advance the fourth letter of the bottom row by one place in the alphabet
&	Add the letter K between the fourth and fifth letters of the top row
╫	Reverse the whole of the top row
♣	Reverse the last three letters of the top row
Ω	Exchange the first and last letters of the bottom row

Example: G W P T A L M
          K S R O P T A F → ♣ + ♫ + Σ
Answer: G W K T M L A
          P S R P P T A F

Explanation:

Stage 1: ♣ Reverse the last three letters of the top row
G W P T M L A
K S R O P T A F

Stage 2: ♫ Exchange the third letter of the top row with first letter of the bottom row
G W K T M L A
P S R O P T A F

Stage 3: ∑ Advance the fourth letter of the bottom row by one place in the alphabet
G W K T M L A
P S R P P T A F

Now try the following five questions (Target time: 10 minutes)

1.
E L P Y N Z X R B
D R U Y Z L M X   →   Ω + ♣ + ♫ + &

2.
S A L I S B U R Y
C A T H E D R A L   →   ╬ + ♣ + Ω + &

3.
Y H C R W Q L N B
P D N T U A S B C T   →   & + Ω + ♣ + ╬

4.
P R E H I S T O R I C
A R C H A E O L O G Y   →   ∑ + & + Ω + ╬ + ♫

5.
G H R T C V B P L E A Q
F P Y R N C X Z U H E L →   ♣ + & + ╬ + ♫ + &

THINKING VERBALLY

1.
The Good, The Bad and The Ugly

In each of the following puzzles four words are listed. You have to find the keyword for which there is a synonym, an antonym and an anagram. For example, if the four words listed are FIRM STEADY RICKETY STAYED, the keyword would be STEADY because the other three words are related to it as follows:

Keyword	Synonym	Antonym	Anagram
STEADY	FIRM	RICKETY	STAYED

Now try the following:

a.
LEAVE CONTINUE REMAIN MARINE
b.
STUNTED SCHOLAR STUDENT TEACHER
c.
ENGRAVE SMOOTH AVENGER ETCH
d.
ADMIRATION SPECTRE CONTEMPT RESPECT
e.
EDUCATION UNAWARENESS INSTRUCTION AUCTIONED
f.
LAMENT MOURN CELEBRATE MANTLE
g.
COASTING SCEPTIC AGNOSTIC BELIEVER
h.
ACCOMPANY FOLLOW SECTOR ESCORT
i.
RESTFUL FLUSTER TENSE RELAXING
j.
ABRUPT RAMBLING TERSE STEER

2.
The clue 'Highly respect apparel' leads to which pair of rhyming words?

3.
Find the starting point and work from letter to letter along the connecting lines to spell out a 13-letter word.

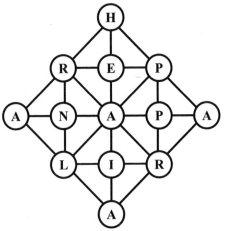

4.
Select two words that are synonyms, plus an antonym of these two synonyms, from the list of words below:

FLAWLESS UNFAIR SPORADIC PLENTIFUL CONSISTENT INTERMITTENT

5.
Change one letter only in each word below to form a familiar phrase:

PLAN FUR TILE

THINKING NUMERICALLY

1.
Which number should replace the question mark?

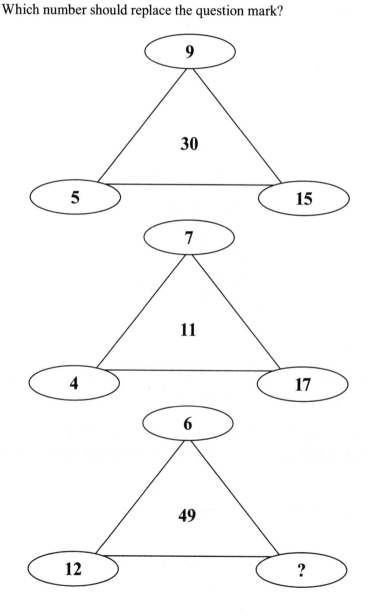

2.
Two numbers are such that if the first receives 60 from the second they are in the ration 2:1, but if the second receives 100 from the first the ratio is 1:3. What are the two numbers?

3.
Number Series

a.

1, 6, 13, 22, 27, 34, ?

What number should replace the question mark to continue the sequence?

b.
In the two numerical sequences below, one number that appears in the top sequence should appear in the bottom sequence and vice versa. Which two numbers should be changed round?

6, 9, 14, 24, 36, 51

2, 4, 8, 15, 22, 32

c.
In the two numerical sequences below, one number that appears in the top sequence should appear in the bottom sequence and vice versa. Which two numbers should be changed round?

10, 25, 41, 54, 76

9, 22, 37, 58, 73

THINKING LOGICALLY

1.

A   C   G   I   M   O   ?

What letter comes next?

2.
An electrical circuit wiring a set of four lights depends on a system of switches A, B, C and D. Each switch when working has the following effect on the lights:

> Switch A turns lights 1 and 2 on/off or off/on
> Switch B turns lights 2 and 4 on/off or off/on
> Switch C turns lights 1 and 3 on/off or off/on
> Switch D turns lights 3 and 4 on/off or off/on

> ○ = ON   ● = OFF

In the following, switches C, A, B and D are thrown in turn, with the result that Set 1 is transformed into Set 2. One of the switches is not, therefore, working and has had no effect on the numbered lights. Identify which one of the switches is not working.

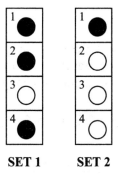

SET 1   SET 2

BRAIN WORKOUT TEN
THINKING LOGICALLY

3.

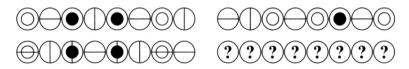

The top set of eight circles has a relationship to the set of eight circles below. The two sets of eight circles on the left have the same relationship as the two sets of eight circles on the right.

Which set of circles should, therefore, replace the question marks?

A

B

C

D

E

THINKING LATERALLY AND CREATIVELY

1.

RAREBIT, JOCULAR, VENISON, SUGARED

What comes next: **LIBERAL**, **CAMELOT**, **LINOCUT**
or **CAPITOL**?

2.
Which number is the odd one out?

$$\quad 2223 \qquad 999996 \qquad 51$$
$$\quad 33334 \qquad 444445 \qquad 112$$

3.

What number should replace the question mark?

4.
What links the following words?

FADE   ERMINE   THRILL   AMAZED
MARZIPAN   DAZZLE   FREEZE   BRAVADO

5.

A E F H I K L M ? ? V W X Y Z

Which two letters are missing?

6.

	12			
	22		?	25
31		33		
41				45
	?			

What two numbers should replace the question marks?

THINKING SPATIALLY

1.

How many triangles appear in the figure below?

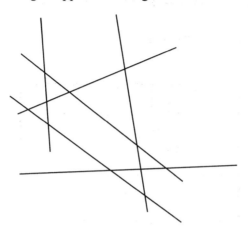

2.

?

Which figure should replace the question mark?

A   B   C   D

THINKING SPATIALLY

3.

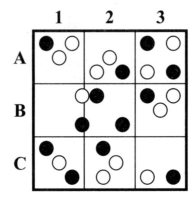

Looking at lines across and down, if the first two tiles are combined to produce the third tile, with the exception that like symbols are cancelled out, which of the above tiles is incorrect, and with which of the tiles below should it be replaced?

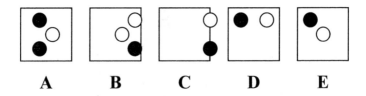

MEMORY

1.

Study the above set of symbols for two minutes, then wait for one minute, and then turn to the next page.

2.

?		▲	
□	!		⊣
☺		╪	
	♫	●	

Study the above for two minutes, then turn to the next page.

BRAIN WORKOUT TEN
MEMORY

1.

i. Which two symbols have changed places?

ii. Which new symbol has been introduced?

When you have an answer to each question, turn back to see if you are correct.

2.

!		▲	
■	?		⊣∣
☺		∓	
	♫	●	£

i. Which two symbols have changed places?

ii. Which symbol has changed from white to black?

iii. Which new symbol has been introduced?

When you have an answer to each question, turn back to see if you are correct.

Any numerical questions should be solved without the aid of a calculator. (Time limit 45 minutes)

1.

$$W \heartsuit \sum \clubsuit - X \$ N$$

Study the above for one minute, then turn to the bottom of the next page.

2.

0.5, 1.25, ? , 2.75, 3.5, 4.25

What number should replace the question mark?

3.
What day and date comes 48 days after Saturday 19 July?

4.

K L M N O P Q R S T

What letter is two places before the letter which is four places after the letter which is two places after the letter M?

5.
Which is the odd one out?

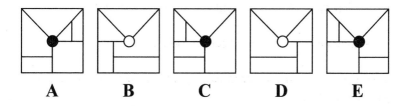

A   **B**   **C**   **D**   **E**

6.
CURABLE SCORE is an anagram of which two words that are opposite in meaning?

7.
How old are Ann and Dan if Ann is now four times as old as Dan but in six years' time will only be twice as old as Dan?

8.
Arrange the following words into alphabetical order:

ABDICATE   ABATTOIR   ABERRANT AARDVARK   ABJECTLY   ABSINTHE ABDUCTOR

9.

3 F G 4 K 9 N T C E J 2 S

Arrange the letters in forward alphabetical order, followed by the numbers in descending order.

10.
419273, 37294, 4973, 794, ?

What comes next?

Question:
Which letter immediately follows the thick black line?

Answers

THINKING QUICKLY

1.
| ☼ | 3 |

2.
| ♪ | 3 |

3.
| ♥ | 2 |

4.
| Ω | 4 |

5.
| ▫ | 2 |

6.
| © | 3 |

7.
| ♦ | 2 |

8.
| β | 6 |

9.
| Ӏ | 2 |

10.
| ☺ | 3 |

THINKING VERBALLY

1.
DAMSON, QUINCE, CHERRY, ORANGE
Reading clockwise from the top left, the shaded squares contain the letters DAMINRNA, which is an anagram of MANDARIN.

2.
HAVE A MEMORY LIKE A SIEVE

3.
ACETIC, RACEME, SPACED, MENACE
The three letters appearing in each word are A, C, and E

4.
BADGER: TUB, SEA, BID, RIG, DUE, FAR

THINKING NUMERICALLY

1.

1	5	2	9	7
9	13	10	17	15
7	11	8	15	13
11	15	12	19	17
6	10	7	14	12

Rows across are progressing +4, -3, +7, -2. Columns down are progressing +8, -2, +4, -5.

2.

1	5	20	27	30	24
8	12	27	34	37	31
20	24	39	46	49	43
11	15	30	37	40	34
19	23	38	45	48	42
25	29	44	51	54	48

Rows across are progressing +4, +15, +7, +3, -6. Columns down are progressing +7, +12, -9, +8, +6.

THINKING LOGICALLY

1.
D: At each stage the black dot moves two places anti-clockwise, the line moves two places clockwise and the white circle moves one place anti-clockwise.

2.
b. the symbols are being repeated, however, a new symbol is always added before the black dash.

3.
d. One card suit is knocked off each time, then added back on. Each set of suits is followed by an arrow in the order ←↑→↓

4.
d. the sequence is repeated after each black line, but with black/white dot reversal.

THINKING LATERALLY AND CREATIVELY

1.

§	♫
#	Σ

The pattern is created by repeating the symbols Σ ♫ § #: in the same order starting at the bottom left-hand corner and working along the bottom row, then back along the next row, etc.

2.
P: So that the alternate letters spell FRANCE - PARIS

3.
3688: In the others multiply the first and fourth digits to obtain the number formed by the middle two digits.

4.
The vowels A E I O U, to produce: ROADS, BELOW, ALIAS, CANOE and SUAVE.

5.
2: Opposite sides on a die always total 7. On 8 dice, therefore, opposite faces total 7 x 8 = 56. As the totals on one side are 40, the total on the opposite sides is 56 – 40 = 16, and 16 ÷ 8 = 2.

THINKING SPATIALLY

1.
C: the rest are all the same figure rotated

2.
Six

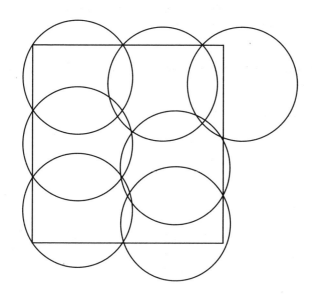

3.
B

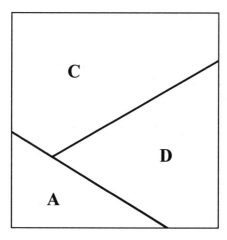

THINKING QUICKLY

Word/symbol speed exercise

1. HALO   2. LOYAL   3. TOWN   4. TALENT   5. ACHE

Letter/Number Rearrangement Exercise

i.   B F J K S T Y 7 6 5 4 2
ii.   B D E G L S Z 9 8 2
iii.   A C E G H L M R U 8 7 5 3 2
iv.   A B D J M S T U Z 9 8 6 4 3
v.   C D G P R S U W X Y 7 6 4 3 2

THINKING VERBALLY

Word Change Exercise

1.
The electricity is passed to the **plug** leads by the top of the rotor arm, driven by the **engine** crankshaft.

2.
Florida is an example of a large **peninsula** as it is surrounded on three sides by water but still attached to a larger **landmass**.

3.
Originally made in Staffordshire, it is **reputedly** named after Toby Philpot, a character in an 18th-century ballad.

4.
Thermistors are used in **lamp** filaments and **electric** motors to stop **large** currents flowing through them when they are initially turned on.

5.
A **natural** resource, such as coal or oil, that takes thousands or millions of years to form and can, therefore not be **replaced** once it is **consumed** is referred to as a non-renewable resource.

Crossword

¹P	R	²I	O	³R		⁴S		⁵S	
A		T		⁶O	P	A	R	T	
⁷S	W	I	S	S		T		A	
S		N		⁸Y	O	U	N	G	
		E				R			
⁹S	C	R	A	¹⁰P		A		¹¹B	
U		A		¹²L	A	T	E	R	
¹³C	O	N	D	O		E		A	
H		T		¹⁴T	O	D	A	Y	

THINKING NUMERICALLY

1.
Addition Exercise

+	7	15	9	23
8	15	23	17	31
13	20	28	22	36
6	13	21	15	29
17	24	32	26	40
26	33	41	35	49
31	38	46	40	54
19	26	34	28	42

2.
26

3.
4225 square yards. Each side will be 65 yards long.
Area = 65 x 65 = 4225.

4.
95 (74 + 21)

5.
£26.95:   (Train £ 17.55, Taxi £ 7.80, Bus £1.60)

6.
700: (98 ÷ 14) x 100

THINKING LOGICALLY

1.
HORSE: Each word starts with the second and fourth letters of the
previous word.

2.
b. Odd numbers are minus 1 and even numbers plus 1.

3.
42: Take the difference between alternate digits, so the difference
between 9 and 5 is 4, and the difference between 1 and 3 is 2.

4.
C: The dot is moving 45 degrees clockwise at each stage, the line in the
large circle is moving 90 degrees clockwise and the line in the middle
circle is moving 45 degrees anti-clockwise.

THINKING LATERALLY AND CREATIVELY

1.
K: to spell BACK TO FRONT starting from the end.

2.
They all have their letters in alphabetical order

Symbolic Odd One Out Puzzles

1.
b. a is the same as c in reverse and d is the same as e in reverse

2.
d. the rest all contain the same five symbols

3.
a. The rest all have the arrows in the same order, albeit stating at a different arrow.

THINKING SPATIALLY

1.
1C

2.
14

3.
E: Each set of lines moves 45 degrees clockwise.

THINKING QUICKLY

Find the Missing Symbol Exercise

1.
b.
& $ F ▶ ♣ ♪ & $ (F) ▶ ♣ ♪ & $ F ▶ ♣ ♪ & $ F ▶ ♣ ♪ & $ F ▶ ♣ ♪ & $
F ▶ ♣ ♪

2.
a.

Find the Letter Exercise
1. F   2. B   3. D   4. H   5. C

THINKING VERBALLY

1.
The letter U converts PONY to PUNY

2.
HISTORY MYSTERY

3.
RILL (a small stream) to produce THRILL, DRILL, TRILL, FRILL,
GRILL and SHRILL.

4.
Synonyms: SLAPDASH, PERFUNCTORY
Antonym: PUNCTILIOUS

5.
Tobago, Antigua

6.
Bed and Breakfast

7.
NUMERICAL

8.
MEOPLC = COMPEL

THINKING NUMERICALLY

1.

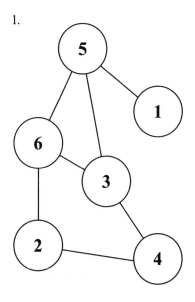

2.
336: 1064 ÷ 19 = 56, and 56 x 6 = 336.

3.
Three: 4872, 2751 and 6993.

4.

8	÷	4	x	3	=	6
+		x		−		−
1	+	3	+	2	=	6
÷		÷		+		+
3	x	4	−	5	=	7
=		=		=		=
3	÷	3	+	6	=	7

THINKING LOGICALLY

1.
A: Pyramids are being constructed by adding a dot to the bottom and then the top alternately. The first dot remains black throughout.

2.
G: The sequence progresses ABcDefGhijKlmnoPqrstuV

3.
4931785
The numbers change places with each other as follows:

A	B	C	D	E	F	G
4	8	5	6	3	9	2
8	7	3	4	5	9	1

D	F	C	G	B	A	E
6	9	5	2	8	4	3
4	9	3	1	7	8	5

4.
C: The first four circles change places with the second four circles.

THINKING LATERALLY AND CREATIVELY

1.
2: The second column is the first column in reverse less 1. The fourth column is the third column in reverse less 1.

2.
They start and finish with the directions NE, SE, SW, NW.

3.
12: Three of each.

4.
The theme is golf, and the words are: score, cart, ball, swing, glove, flag, drive, club, course, range.

5.
Just one: the black in the middle. All the rest are incomplete circles. Only one circle actually appears.

THINKING SPATIALLY

1.

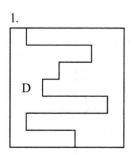

2.
D

THINKING QUICKLY

1.

a.

☼♥▼▲◄—●☺☼♥♀☼♥▼▲◄—●☺☼♥♀☼♥▼▲◄—●☼♥♀☼♥▼(
▲)◄—●☺☼♥♀☼♥▼▲◄—●☺☼♥♀

2.

E

3.

Letter/Code Change Exercise

1. M N L Z H U T H J S P P C

2. G T H H L P W Y M

3. H E A H D P L J B RY P C

4. C P G R P J C R H E L T

5. R Z S M B T P U H F D P C

THINKING VERBALLY

1.

COMBINE

2.

Synonyms: PLETHORA, GLUT

Antonym: DEARTH

3.
a. LO(CAT)ION
b. ENV(IRON)MENT
c. COM(PARIS)ON
d. CONS(TRAIN)T
e. HAP(PINE)SS

4.

H	E	A	P	S
E	Q	U	A	L
A	U	D	I	O
P	A	I	N	T
S	L	O	T	H

THINKING NUMERICALLY

Complete the Equation Exercise

1. D

2. A

3. C

4. D

5. A

6. B

THINKING LOGICALLY

1.
C: Looking across add a cross, looking down add a small circle.

2.
c. The sequence consists of the repeated symbols ╬ ╦ ╫ ╬ ╗╠ preceded by ♫ and ♪ alternately.

3.
a. Deduct 2 from the first three numbers and add 2 to the second three numbers.

THINKING LATERALLY AND CREATIVELY

1.
354: The first digit of the middle number is produced by dividing the top number by 2, the second is produced by dividing the bottom left number by 3 and the third digit is produced by dividing the bottom right number by 4.

2. Verbosities

i.   Boring the pants off someone.

ii. Getting hold of the wrong end of the stick.

iii. Starting the ball rolling.

3.
November: In the NATO alphabet, Q = Quebec, H = hotel, G = golf, T = tango, J = Juliet and N = November.

THINKING SPATIALLY

1.
B and D

2.
B, C and D

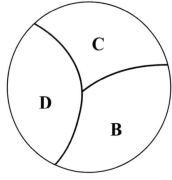

3.
8

THINKING QUICKLY

1.
1. MANIFOLD, ABUNDANT

2. CULPABLE, INNOCENT

3. DILIGENT, CARELESS

4. SURROUND, ENCIRCLE

THINKING VERBALLY

1.
INEPTLY

2.
Tit for tat

3.
LEOPARD: NIL, RUE, AGO, RIP, PEA, JAR, LAD

4.
Fair and Square

5.
LEGACY, CYMBAL, ALLURE, RETAIN, INCOME, MEDDLE

6.

S	I	N	C	E	R	E
N		A		V		R
A	N	I	M	A	T	E
R		V		D		C
E	L	E	M	E	N	T

THINKING NUMERICALLY

1.
Multiplication Exercise

x	3	9	7	12	8
6	18	54	42	72	48
13	39	117	91	156	104
5	15	45	35	60	40
11	33	99	77	132	88
12	36	108	84	144	96
8	24	72	56	96	64
14	42	126	98	168	112
25	75	225	175	300	200

2.
12

3.
Starter   =   1 unit   £3.00
Dessert   =   2 units   £6.00
Main course =   4 units   £12.00
                          7 units   £21.00
£21.00 divided by 7 = £3 per unit

4.
25 and 15: There are two alternate sequences: the first starting at 0 progresses +3, and the second starting at 1 progresses + 3, +5, +7, +9

5.
7

THINKING LOGICALLY

1.
0: In the top line in each box the numbers increase by 2, in the second line by 3 and in the bottom line by 4.

2.
10: In the left-hand box the numbers in each line across, down and corner to corner total 12, and in the right-hand box they total 18.

3.
7: 812- 583 = 229 and 769 – 597 = 172

4.
8: Looking down each line, 196 + 381 = 577 and 287 + 596 = 883

5.
7: In each line across, add the first two numbers less 1 to obtain the third number.

THINKING LATERALLY AND CREATIVELY

1.
0: Looking across and down the sum of the first two numbers in each line and column totals the second two numbers, eg 3 + 2 = 4 + 1

2.
MOHAIR, ACT
The rest can be paired so that three-letter words can be spelled out by the alternate letters of the six-letter words: TRYING/RIG, HOWLED/OLD, NEARER/ERR, MISCUE/ICE, POODLE/ODE.

3.
D: Looking across, the top left-hand corner alternates white dot/black dot; in the top right-hand corner the white dot moves round one corner clockwise at each stage; in the bottom left-hand corner the line alternates horizontal/vertical, and in the bottom right-hand corner the line moves one corner clockwise at each stage.

4.
c. The arrows either side of the face are reversed.

5.
d. The rest contain the same eight symbols. In d the symbol Ψ is substituted by ♀.

THINKING SPATIALLY

1.
D

2.
D: in all the others the left half is an exact mirror-image of the right half

3.
14

THINKING QUICKLY

1.
Letter and Number Arrangement Exercise

i.
2 4 6 9 T N M L K E D C
ii.
3 5 6 7 9 Z T S P M J F D
iii.
3 5 7 8 9 X U T Q N H F D C A
iv.
2 4 5 6 8 X W U S Q L J G F B A
v.
2 5 6 8 Y X U T S Q P L K J G E B

2.
Fives:

S	H	E	L	F		E		E	N	S	U	E
H		N		I	N	D	E	X		A		N
Y	O	D	E	L		I		U	R	B	A	N
L		U		E	X	C	E	L		O		U
Y	I	E	L	D		T		T	U	T	T	I
	S		I					P		H		
P	S	A	L	M				S	P	O	U	T
	U		A					E		M		
T	E	A	C	H		C		P	R	O	B	E
O		T		O	T	H	E	R		V		N
A	L	L	O	T		U		E	N	A	C	T
S		A		L	I	T	H	E		T		R
T	A	S	T	Y		E		N	E	E	D	Y

THINKING VERBALLY

1.
ANATHEMA: to produce PLAN/ANEW, WHAT/ATOM, ACHE/HEAT, PUMA/MARK

2.
Theme Puzzles
i. PHEASANT
ii. PISCES
iii. SWEATER

3.
Noughts and Crosswords
i. Chiv**alr**y, G**arla**nd
ii. I**nep**t, Car**pen**ter
iii. U**pli**ft, Sai**lp**lane
iv. **Gia**nt, **Sna**il

THINKING NUMERICALLY

1.

5	+	7	÷	4	=	3
−		−		+		−
3	x	4	÷	6	=	2
x		+		÷		+
2	÷	2	+	5	=	6
=		=		=		=
4	+	5	−	2	=	7

2.
11: add 0.5, then deduct, 0.75, then add 1, then deduct 1.25, then add 1.5

3.
14 cases   238 x 2 = 476   476 ÷ 34 = 14

4.
34 minutes
12 noon less 34 minutes = 11.26
11.26 less 18 minutes = 11.08
10.00 am plus 68 minutes (2 x 34) = 11.08

5.
631524 or 425136

6.
Phil £360 and Jill £280

THINKING LOGICALLY

1.
72 (9 x 9) - 9

2.
838: Each digit is increased by 1 in turn, from last to first.

3.
Switch C is faulty

4.
B: The first four circles change places with the second four circles

THINKING LATERALLY AND CREATIVELY

1.
521646
In all the others multiply each pair of digits to obtain the next digit/s in the sequence, eg 7 x 4 = 28, 2 x 8 = 16, to produce 742816.

2.
V: To give the phrase A CUT ABOVE.

3.
167
1728 ÷ 12 = 144
 144 ÷ 12 = 12
  12 ÷ 12 =   1
            ———
            167

4.
8: Add the first and second, then third and fourth numbers in rows 1 and 3 to obtain the number below. For example, in row three 8 + 5 = 13 and 9 + 9 = 18. Similarly in row one 3 + 9 = 12 and 7 + 6 = 13.

5.
7: In each straight row of four numbers alternate digits total the same, ie 17 + 12 (29) = 14 + 15 (29); 3 + 16 (19) = 14 + 5 (19), etc.

THINKING SPATIALLY

1.

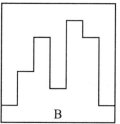

2.
E

THINKING QUICKLY

Find the Missing Symbol Exercise

1.
d.
○○○●●○●○●●○●○○○●●○○○●●○●○●●○○○●●○○○●●○●○●●○○(○○)●●●○○○
●●○●●○●○○○●●○○○●●○●●○●○○○●●●

2.
b. (every fourth figure is larger than the rest)

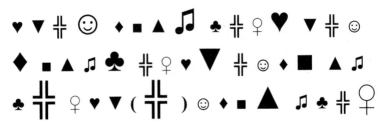

Find the Letter Exercise

1. L   2. Y   3. Q   4. J   5. Z

THINKING VERBALLY

1.
AT BINGO = BOATING
The rivers are: EUPHRATES (SUPERHEAT), DANUBE (BENAUD), MEKONG (GONK ME), SEVERN (NERVES), NIAGARA (NAG ARIA)

2.
a. Slick trick   b. Terse curse   c. Nude prude   d. Endorse Norse

3.

L	E	A	P			P	A	S	T
E	R	G	O			A	B	L	E
A	G	U	E			S	L	U	R
P	O	E	M	I	S	T	E	R	M
			I	D	E	A			
			S	E	A	M			
C	A	R	T	A	M	E	A	C	H
A	R	I	A			A	X	L	E
R	I	S	K			C	L	U	E
T	A	K	E			H	E	E	D

THINKING NUMERICALLY

1.

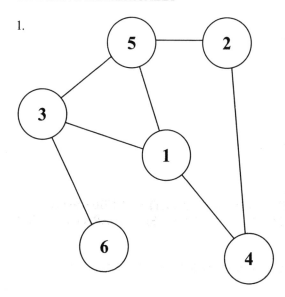

2.
283: Multiply by 3 and add 1 at each stage.

3.
Seven punnets each containing 17 strawberries.

4.
46
Combined age in 5 years = 54
Combined age now = 54 – (4 x 5) = 34
Combined age in 3 years = 34 + (4 x 3) = 46

5.
Jane 32 and Cain 24
When Jane was 24, Cain was 16 (ie half the age that Jane is now)

6.
£140: Jim had 2/5 and Alf 20% = 1/5 (total 3/5), therefore the remaining £56 that Sid had must be the remaining two fifths. One fifth, therefore, must equal £28 and the total amount of money must be 28 x 5 = 140.

THINKING LOGICALLY

1.
E: A black circle is always opposite a circle with a horizontal line, a white circle is always opposite a circle with a vertical line.

2.
40: (8 x 2 x 3) - 8

3.
87: x5 -1, x5 – 2, x5 -3, x5 – 4, x5 – 5, x5 - 6

4.
e. Multiply the number formed by the top six digits by 2. ie 289643 x 2 = 579286 and 482937 x 2 = 965874.

THINKING LATERALLY AND CREATIVELY

1.
They are anagrams of countries: Spain, Cyprus, Nepal, Iran, China, Italy.

2.
12: Add the first three digits and then deduct the last: $(2 + 8 + 3) - 1 = 12$

3.
6: Looking across each line $36 \div 2 = 18$, $94 \div 2 = 47$, $68 \div 2 = 34$ and $52 \div 2 = 26$

4.

The pattern repeats ╫F├╢╤‖ in the same order starting at the bottom left corner and working up the first column, then down the second, etc.

THINKING SPATIALLY

1.
The pads should be visited in the following order:

8	5	1
6	*	3
4	2	7

2.
C: Lines continue from square to square horizontally and vertically.

3.
3C is incorrect.

THINKING QUICKLY

Double Letter/Code Change Exercise

1.
DKATKRUSPB
ARYVLXZON

2.
DOSEKRMANN
BINSCHERP

3.
CIPOBRKEPYH
LARBBOLOID

4.
FGQAPMYTR
PWESTYUIOO

5.
ELEAKIFITJUS
BXPFCTATION

Word Change Exercise

1.
In human pre-history, the only power **available** was muscle power, **augmented** by primitive tools, such as the wedge or lever.

2.
Your **printer** must be set up as a shared printer on the **computer** to which it is connected before you access it from another computer.

3.
When there are two main parties, divided along class lines, the one gaining **power** can often undo the **legislation** of its predecessor.

THINKING VERBALLY

1.
WEAK, STRONG

2.
ANY OLD HOW

3.
MICROPROCESSOR

4.

¹S	A	²B	O	³T		⁴A	
U		O		⁵U	N	F	I	⁶T
⁷C	O	W	E	R		T		R
C				F		E		A
⁸I	O	⁹T	A		¹⁰G	R	I	N
N		O		¹¹E				S
C		A		¹²V	E	¹³N	O	M
¹⁴T	A	S	T	E		A		I
		T		¹⁵N	I	G	H	T

THINKING NUMERICALLY

1.
27: the sequence progresses -15, -14, -15, -14, -15

2.
Jim 27, Alf 36, Sid 48, Mary 64.

3.
280: (462 ÷ 1.65)

4.
1 hour 16 minutes

5.
3: Total of 3 numbers 19 x 3 = 57, and total of 2 numbers 27 x 2 = 54, so
57 – 54 = 3

6.
b.

7.
15 and 16 should be interchanged. The first sequence progresses +3, +5,
+7, +9, +11, and the second sequence progresses +2, +4, +6, +8, +10.

THINKING LOGICALLY

1.
5968: In all the others the digits progress +4, -2, +3

2.
158: In each block of four numbers (as in the example below) the bottom
right-hand number is the total of the other three, ie 3 + 1 + 4 = 8:

3	1
4	8

3.

Looking across, the line is moving 45 degrees clockwise. Looking down
it is moving 45 degrees anti-clockwise.

4.
B: Each pair of circles swap round.

THINKING LATERALLY AND CREATIVELY

1.
She cat/Chic hat

2.
3690: 6 x 2 x 3 = 36 and 5 x 9 x 2 = 90

3.

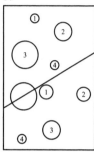

4.
C: The circles all move on two places.

THINKING SPATIALLY

1.
D: It spirals anti-clockwise; the rest spiral clockwise.

2.
A: The rest are the same figure rotated.

3.

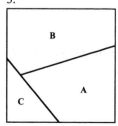

THINKING QUICKLY

Anagrammed Synonym Test

a. QUESTIONABLE – DUBIOUS
b. CHARACTER – TRAIT
c. TOURNAMENT – CONTEST
d. COOPERATE – ASSIST
e. UNDERNEATH – BELOW

Word/symbol speed exercise

1. CLOWN, 2. ICILY, 3. PANIC, 4. CHAPLAIN, 5. OWLET

THINKING VERBALLY

1.
FIGHT and PLAY

a. Rough and Tumble   b. Lost and Found
c. Rock and Roll   d. Touch and Go
e. Supply and Demand   f. Chapter and Verse
g. Hammer and Tongs   h. Fast and Furious
i. Bright and Early   j. Pros and Cons

2.
Synonyms: PRINCIPAL, PARAMOUNT
Antonym: AUXILIARY

3.
ANTICYCLONE, TEMPERATURE, THUNDERCLAP,
METEOROLOGY
Reading clockwise from the top left, the shaded squares contain
the letters AIONULCRD, which is an anagram of RAINCLOUD.

THINKING NUMERICALLY

1.

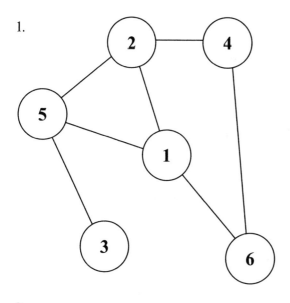

2.
10: the sequence progresses -9, -18, -27, -36

3.
4: In each block of four numbers the sum of two diagonals equals the product of the other two diagonals, for example 4 + 8 = 6 x 2.

4.
49 minutes: 11.11am less 22 minutes = 10.49am, 10.00am plus 49 minutes = 10.49am.

5.
23: (7x3) + 2

THINKING LOGICALLY

1.
35 and 110: 7 x 5 = 35; 75 + 35 = 110. Similarly 2 x 9 = 18, 29 + 18 = 47, 4 x 7 = 28, etc.

2.
d. the arrows between the black dots consist of a repeated sequence except that, working from left to right one arrow is rotating 90 degrees clockwise in turn.

3.
c. add pairs of numbers on the top row to obtain each pair on the bottom row, ie 8 + 9 = 17, 6 + 5 = 11 and 7 + 8 = 15.

4.
A: A black dot is always opposite a vertical line and a white dot is always opposite a horizontal line.

THINKING LATERALLY AND CREATIVELY

1.
K L M N

2.
8: Multiply the digits of each number to obtain the next.

3.

The top row contains circles, the second row triangles and the third row squares. In each line across and down, one symbol is shaded black.

4.
3: each number describes the number of other numbers that are immediately adjacent to it horizontally, vertically and diagonally.

5.
Horatio (HO ratio)

THINKING SPATIALLY

1.

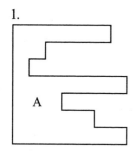

2.
Six

3.

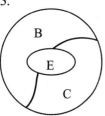

THINKING QUICKLY

Anagrammed Synonyms and Antonyms Exercise

1.
ATTEST, CERTIFY

2.
DEDUCE, CONCLUDE

3.
SPORTING, UNFAIR

4.
FEW, NUMEROUS

Double Letter/Code Change Exercise

1.
ELXYKNZBRX
PRUYZLMD

2.
YRUBKSISAL
LATHEDRAC

3.
LNBQWKRCHY
TDNTUASBCP

4.
CIYOTSIKHERP
RRCIAEOLOGA

5.
EAFLKPBVCKTRHG
QPYRNCXZUHEL

THINKING VERBALLY

1. The Good, The Bad and The Ugly

Keyword	Synonym	Antonym	Anagram
a. REMAIN	CONTINUE	LEAVE	MARINE
b. STUDENT	SCHOLAR	TEACHER	STUNTED
c. ENGRAVE	ETCH	SMOOTH	AVENGER
d. RESPECT	ADMIRATION	CONTEMPT	SPECTRE
e. EDUCATION	INSTRUCTION	UNAWARENESS	AUCTIONED
f. LAMENT	MOURN	CELEBRATE	MANTLE
g. AGNOSTIC	SCEPTIC	BELIEVER	COASTING
h. ESCORT	ACCOMPANY	FOLLOW	SECTOR
i. RESTFUL	RELAXING	TENSE	FLUSTER
j. TERSE	ABRUPT	RAMBLING	STEER

2.
ADMIRE ATTIRE

3.
PARAPHERNALIA

4.
Synonyms: SPORADIC, INTERMITTENT
Antonym: CONSISTENT

5.
PLAY FOR TIME

THINKING NUMERICALLY

1.
23: $(6 \times 12) - 23 = 49$

2.
196 and 188

3.
Number Series
a.
43: The sequence progresses +5, +7, +9, +5, +7, +9

b.
14 and 15 should be interchanged.
The top sequence progresses +3, +6, +9, +12, +15
The bottom sequence progresses +2, +4, +6, +8, +10

c.
54 and 58 should be interchanged.
The top sequence progresses +15, +16, +17, +18
The bottom sequence progresses +13, +15, +17, +19

THINKING LOGICALLY

1.
S: The sequence progresses: AbCdefGhIjklMnOpqrS

2.
Switch B is faulty.

3.
E: A small white circle is always opposite a small white circle with an horizontal line, an horizontal line is always opposite a vertical line, a black dot is always opposite a black dot with a vertical line.

THINKING LATERALLY AND CREATIVELY

1.
LINOCUT: the vowels AEIOU are being repeated in the same order.

2.
999996: In all the other numbers the last number describes the number of times that the first digit is repeated.

3.
8: The numbers in each circle total 20.

4.
Animals: FA(DE, ER)MINE, THRI(LL, AMA)ZED,
MARZI(PAN, DA)ZZLE, FREE(ZE, BRA)VADO

5.
NT: A list of letters in the English alphabet made up of straight lines.

6.
24 and 52: Each number describes its position in the grid, ie the number
12 is on row 1, column 2.

THINKING SPATIALLY

1.
Six

2.
C: The figure is rotating 90 degrees clockwise at each stage.

3.
Tile 3B is incorrect and should be replaced by tile D.

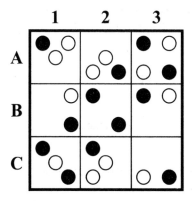

1.
57: add 19 at each stage

2.
NEVIOC = novice

3.
C and G should be changed round: the line moves 45 degrees clockwise at each stage.

4.
24: This will make the sequence palindromic, ie it will read the same backwards and forwards.

5.
11

6.
Ideal meal

7.
One mile east

8.
434

9.
TUBS: the letters all move forward one place in the alphabet.

10.
LEAF: the words end with the letters A, B, C, D, E, F.

Score one point for each correct answer.

Work out your percentage score by dividing the score obtained by the number of questions and multiplying by 100. Round up to the nearest whole number and plot the percentage score obtained on the progress graph at the end of the book.

1.
May: Miss three months then one month alternately.

2.
Loot/lute

3.
37.5: Deduct 7.5, 10, 12.5, 15, 17.5
(the amount deducted increases by 2.5 each time).

4.
PMTJC. The letters move: 1 2 3 4 5   5 3 2 4 1
                         C T M J P   P M T J C

5.
b. 956

6.
Wednesday

7.
D: The first three figures are being repeated as mirror images.

8.
Cure, remedy

9.
VIII, V, III, XII, X

10.
Tom 336, Dick 224, Harriet 112

Score one point for each correct answer.

Work out your percentage score by dividing the score obtained by the number of questions and multiplying by 100. Round up to the nearest whole number and plot the percentage score obtained on the progress graph at the end of the book.

1.
C: The rest are the same figure rotated.

2.
3 9 Y X N M L K G F B 6 4 2

3.
Clubs

4.
Obstacle, Barrier

5.
s: Looking across miss two letters then one letter then three letters.
Looking down: miss one letter, then two then three.

6.
less: Pair the first four words with the second four words to produce
passport, wayward, carpet and hopeless.

7.
Synonyms: Binding, Obligatory
Antonym: Optional

8.
71: deduct 5 then 7 alternately.

9.
c. In all the others the first half is a mirror-image of the second half.

10.
1 metre: 1 metre sapling + 3 metres fence = 4 metres.

Score one point for each correct answer.

Work out your percentage score by dividing the score obtained by the
number of questions and multiplying by 100. Round up to the nearest
whole number and plot the percentage score obtained on the progress
graph at the end of the book.

1.
KNOT: BFGJ**KNOT**VWYZ

2.
c. The list consists of the repeated symbols: ╫ Ω ♣ Ξ ♫ ∏

╫ Ω ♣ Ξ ♫ ∏ ╫ Ω ♣ Ξ ♫ ∏ ╫ Ω ♣ (Ξ) ♫ ∏ ╫ Ω ♣ Ξ ♫ ∏

3.
B: At each stage the white and black dots move 180 degrees and the line moves 45 degrees clockwise.

4.
42

5.
MAT

6.
813: In all the others the digits total 11.

7.
CAT: Copycat, polecat, catnap and catcall.

8.
Q: AbcdEfgHiJklmNopQ

9.
c. HONEY: Each word commences with the last letter of the previous word.

10.
28: Add 3, 4, 5, 6, 7

Score one point for each correct answer.

Work out your percentage score by dividing the score obtained by the number of questions and multiplying by 100. Round up to the nearest whole number and plot the percentage score obtained on the progress graph at the end of the book.

1.
X

2.
2: Add 0.75 at each stage

3.
Friday 5 September

4.
Q

5.
C: A and E are mirror images as are B and D

6.
Clear, Obscure

7.
Ann 12, Dan 3

8.
AARDVARK, ABATTOIR, ABDICATE, ABDUCTOR, ABERRANT,
ABJECTLY, ABSINTHE

9.
CEFGJKNST9432

10.
97: At each stage reverse the previous number and discard the lowest
digit.

Score one point for each correct answer.

Work out your percentage score by dividing the score obtained by the
number of questions and multiplying by 100. Round up to the nearest
whole number and plot the percentage score obtained on the progress
graph at the end of the book.

Use the graph below to plot your progress on the five Progress Tests.

In order for the chart to be effective the Tests should be attempted in the order in which they appear in the book.

Percentage % score

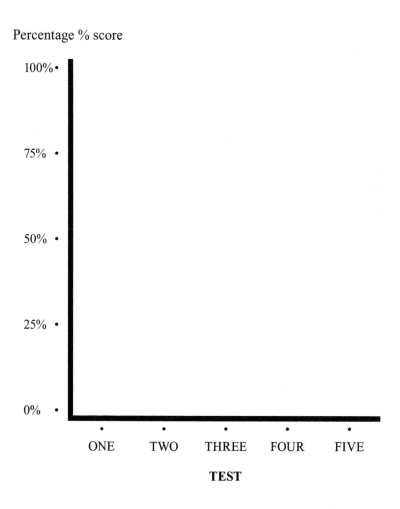

Perfect Babies' Names

Rosalind Fergusson

All you need to choose the ideal name

- Do you want help finding the perfect name?
- Are you unsure whether to go for something traditional or something more unusual?
- Do you want to know a bit more about the names you are considering?

Perfect Babies' Names is an essential resource for all parents-to-be. Taking a close look at over 3,000 names, it not only tells you each name's meaning and history, it also tells you which famous people have shared it over the years and how popular – or unpopular – it is now. With tips on how to make a shortlist and advice for avoiding unfortunate nicknames, *Perfect Babies' Names* is the ultimate one-stop guide.

The *Perfect* series is a range of practical guides that give clear and straightforward advice on everything from getting your first job to choosing your baby's name. Written by experienced authors offering tried-and-tested tips, each book contains all you need to get it right first time.

BOOKS

Perfect Best Man

George Davidson

All you need to know

- Do you want to make sure you're a great best man?
- Do you want to make the groom glad he chose you?
- Do you need some guidance on your role and responsibilities?

Perfect Best Man is an indispensable guide to every aspect of the best man's role. Covering everything from organising the stag night to making sure the big day runs according to plan, it walks you through exactly what you need to do and gives great advice about getting everything done with the least possible fuss. With checklists to make sure you have it all covered, troubleshooting sections for when things go wrong, and a unique chapter on choosing and organising the ushers, *Perfect Best Man* has everything you need to make sure you rise to the occasion.

BOOKS

Perfect Confidence

Jan Ferguson

All you need to get it right first time

- Do you find it hard to stay calm under pressure?
- Are you worried that you don't always stand up for yourself?
- Do you want some straightforward advice on overcoming insecurities?

Perfect Confidence is the ideal companion for anyone who wants to boost their self-esteem. Covering everything from communicating clearly to handling conflict, it explains exactly why confidence matters and equips you with the skills you need to become more assertive. Whether you need to get ahead in the workplace or learn how to balance the demands of friends and family, *Perfect Confidence* has all you need to meet challenges head on.

The *Perfect* series is a range of practical guides that give clear and straightforward advice on everything from getting your first job to choosing your baby's name. Written by experienced authors offering tried-and-tested tips, each book contains all you need to get it right first time.

BOOKS

Perfect CV

Max Eggert

All you need to get it right first time

- Are you determined to succeed in your job search?
- Do you need guidance on how to make a great first impression?
- Do you want to make sure your CV stands out?

Bestselling *Perfect CV* is essential reading for anyone who's applying for jobs. Written by a leading HR professional with years of experience, it explains what recruiters are looking for, gives practical advice about how to show yourself in your best light, and provides real-life examples to help you improve your CV. Whether you're a graduate looking to take the first step on the career ladder, or you're planning an all-important job change, *Perfect CV* will help you stand out from the competition.

BOOKS

Perfect Interview

Max Eggert

All you need to get it right first time

- Are you determined to succeed in your job search?
- Do you want to make sure you have the edge on the other candidates?
- Do you want to find out what interviewers are *really* looking for?

Perfect Interview is an invaluable guide for anyone who's applying for jobs. Written by a leading HR professional with years of experience in the field, it explains how interviews are constructed, gives practical advice about how to show yourself in your best light, and provides real-life examples to help you practise at home. Whether you're a graduate looking to take the first step on the career ladder, or you're planning an all-important job change, *Perfect Interview* will help you stand out from the competition.

BOOKS

Perfect Memory Training

Fiona McPherson

All you need to get it right first time

- Do you sometimes find it hard to remember names, dates or where you left your keys?
- Would you like to find out how your memory works?
- Do you want to learn some simple skills to help you stop forgetting things?

Perfect Memory Training is essential reading for anyone who wants to strengthen their powers of recall. Written by Dr Fiona McPherson, a psychologist with years of experience in the field, it explains how memories are created and stored, sets out a range of techniques to help you improve these processes, and provides exercises to help you track your progress. Whether you want to get better at remembering names, faces, lists or pieces of general knowledge, *Perfect Memory Training* has everything you need to boost your mental ability.

BOOKS

Perfect Numerical Test Results

Joanna Moutafi and Ian Newcombe

All you need to get it right first time

- Have you been asked to sit a numerical reasoning test?
- Do you want guidance on the sorts of questions you'll be asked?
- Do you want to make sure you perform to the best of your abilities?

Perfect Numerical Test Results is the ideal guide for anyone who wants to secure their ideal job. Written by a team from Kenexa, one of the UK's leading compilers of psychometric tests, it explains how numerical tests work, gives helpful pointers on how to get ready, and provides professionally constructed sample questions for you to try out at home. It also contains an in-depth section on online testing – the route that more and more recruiters are choosing to take. Whether you're a graduate looking to take the first step on the career ladder, or you're planning an all-important job change, *Perfect Numerical Test Results* has everything you need to make sure you stand out from the competition.

BOOKS

Perfect Personality Profiles

Helen Baron

All you need to get it right first time

- Have you been asked to complete a personality question-naire?
- Do you need guidance on the sorts of questions you'll be asked?
- Do you want to make sure you show yourself in your best light?

Perfect Personality Profiles is essential reading for anyone who needs to find out more about psychometric profiling. Including everything from helpful pointers on how to get ready to professionally constructed sample questions for you to try out at home, it walks you through every aspect of preparing for a test. Whether you're a graduate looking to take the first step on the career ladder, or you're planning an all-important job change, *Perfect Personality Profiles* has everything you need to make sure you stand out from the competition.

BOOKS

Perfect Positive Thinking

Lynn Williams

All you need to know

- Are you troubled by negative thoughts?
- Do you find it hard to get motivated?
- Would you like some guidance on how to feel more upbeat?

Perfect Positive Thinking is essential reading for anyone who wants to feel optimistic and enthusiastic. Written by a professional life coach, with years of experience in the field, it gives practical advice on how to overcome negative feelings, explains how to deal with problems like anxiety and self-doubt, and provides helpful tips on how to gain energy, motivation and a sense of purpose. Covering everything from exercising to eating, and from stretching to sleep, *Perfect Positive Thinking* has all you need to feel happy and confident.

BOOKS

Perfect Psychometric Test Results

Joanna Moutafi and Ian Newcombe

All you need to get it right first time

- Have you been asked to sit a psychometric test?
- Do you want guidance on the sorts of questions you'll be asked?
- Do you want to make sure you perform to the best of your abilities?

Perfect Psychometric Test Results is an essential guide for anyone who wants to secure their ideal job. Written by a team from Kenexa, one of the UK's leading compilers of psychometric tests, it explains how each test works, gives helpful pointers on how to get ready, and provides professionally constructed sample questions for you to try out at home. It also contains an in-depth section on online testing – the route that more and more recruiters are choosing to take. Whether you're a graduate looking to take the first step on the career ladder, or you're planning an all-important job change, *Perfect Psychometric Test Results* has everything you need to make sure you stand out from the competition.

BOOKS

Perfect Pub Quiz

David Pickering

All you need to stage a great quiz

- Who invented the cat-flap?
- Which is the largest island in the world?
- What is tofu made of?

Perfect Pub Quiz is the ideal companion for all general knowledge nuts. Whether you're organising a quiz night in your local or you simply want to get in a bit of practice on tricky subjects, *Perfect Pub Quiz* has all the questions and answers. With topics ranging from the Roman Empire to *Little Britain* and from the Ryder Cup to Alex Rider, this easy-to-use quiz book will tax your brain and provide hours of fun.

BOOKS

Perfect Punctuation

Stephen Curtis

All you need to get it right first time

- Do you find punctuation a bit confusing?
- Are you worried that your written English might show you up?
- Do you want a simple way to brush up your skills?

Perfect Punctuation is an invaluable guide to mastering punctuation marks and improving your writing. Covering everything from semi-colons to inverted commas, it gives step-by-step guidance on how to use each mark and how to avoid common mistakes. With helpful examples of correct and incorrect usage and exercises that enable you to practise what you've learned, *Perfect Punctuation* has everything you need to ensure that you never make a mistake again.

BOOKS

ALSO AVAILABLE IN RANDOM HOUSE BOOKS

Perfect Readings for Weddings

Jonathan Law

All you need to make your special day perfect

- Do you want your wedding to be that little bit more special?
- Do you want to personalise the ceremony by including readings that are just right for you?
- Do you need help tracking down a traditional reading, or finding something more out of the way?

Perfect Readings for Weddings is an anthology of the best poems, prose passages and quotations about love and marriage. Including everything from familiar blessings and verses to more unusual choices, it covers every sort of reading you could wish for. With advice on how to choose readings that complement one another and tips on how to ensure that everything runs smoothly on the day, *Perfect Readings for Weddings* has everything you need to make sure the whole ceremony is both memorable and meaningful.

BOOKS

Order more titles in the *Perfect* series
from your local bookshop, or have them delivered
direct to your door by Bookpost.

Free post and packing
Overseas customers allow £2 per paperback

Phone: 01624 677237

Post: Random House Books
c/o Bookpost, PO Box 29, Douglas, Isle of Man IM99 1BQ

Fax: 01624 670 923

email: bookshop@enterprise.net

Cheques (payable to Bookpost) and credit cards accepted

Prices and availability subject to change without notice.
Allow 28 days for delivery.
When placing your order, please state if you do not
wish to receive any additional information.

www.rbooks.co.uk

BOOKS